QUICK CASTS:
PORTLAND, OREGON

Help Us Keep This Guide Up to Date

Every effort has been made by the author and editors to make this guide as accurate and useful as possible. However, many things can change after a guide is published—fish populations fluctuate, rules and regulations change, techniques evolve, sites and other facilities come under new management, Mother Nature asserts her will, and so on.

We would appreciate hearing from you concerning your experiences with this guide and how you feel it could be improved and kept up to date. While we may not be able to respond to all comments and suggestions, we'll take them to heart, and we'll also make certain to share them with the author. Please send your comments and suggestions to the following address:

GPP
Reader Response/Editorial Department
P.O. Box 480
Guilford, CT 06437

Or you may e-mail us at:

editorial@globepequot.com

Thanks for your input, and happy angling!

QUICK CASTS:
PORTLAND, OREGON

The Top Fishing Spots within an Hour's Drive of the City

JIM YUSKAVITCH

Lyons Press
Guilford, Connecticut

An imprint of Globe Pequot Press

Design: Sheryl P. Kober
Project editor: Julie Marsh
Layout: Sue Murray
Interior photos: Jim Yuskavitch
Maps by Trailhead Graphics, Inc. © Morris Book Publishing, LLC
TOPO! Explorer software and SuperQuad source maps courtesy of National Geographic Maps. For information about TOPO! Explorer, TOPO!, and Nat Geo Maps products, go to www.topo.com or www.natgeomaps.com.

Library of Congress Cataloging-in-Publication Data

Yuskavitch, James.
  Quick casts : Portland, Oregon : the top fishing spots within an hour's drive of the city / Jim Yuskavitch.
      p. cm. — (Fishing series)
  Summary: "Describes the state's fishing from the tidewaters to the high desert in the east"— Provided by publisher.
  ISBN 978-0-7627-7337-4 (pbk.)
  1. Fishing—Oregon—Portland—Guidebooks.   2. Fly fishing—Oregon—Portland—Guidebooks. I. Title.
  SH539.Y875 2011
  799.109795'49—dc23

                                                                                      2011034651

Printed in the United States of America
10 9 8 7 6 5 4 3 2 1

Contents

Overview

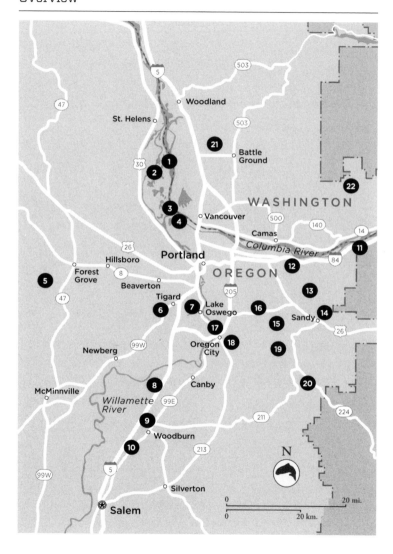

Introduction

Portland, Oregon, is one of the great cities of the Pacific Northwest, and one of the great things about it is the ample selection of high-quality places to fish within a short drive of its bustling downtown core. An angler living in or near Portland is always within striking distance of excellent fishing opportunities for a variety of species. On its northern border is the mighty Columbia River with its runs of salmon and steelhead, along with shad, sturgeon, and a cornucopia of warm-water species. The Willamette River, one of the Columbia's major tributaries, runs right through the city and offers myriad fishing opportunities—in particular, its renowned spring chinook salmon run.

To the west and south of Portland, as well as within city limits and surrounding suburbs, you'll find smaller rivers, along with ponds and reservoirs that provide opportunities to catch a smorgasbord of bass, panfish, and trout. Some of the smaller ponds are great places to introduce kids to fishing. To the east of the city, in the foothills of the Cascade Range, lie some of the best salmon and steelhead streams in the state, including the Sandy and Clackamas Rivers, where you can fish crystal-clear water flowing through deep forests of big trees that give no hint of how close you are to civilization.

This book makes no attempt to cover all the fishing opportunities in the Portland area. Instead, it focuses on some of the signature waters within an hour's drive of the city where you can catch a range of species using a variety of fishing methods. In addition to the basics, such as how to find each river, lake, or pond and the kinds of fish you can catch there, the book also offers some suggestions and tips on gear and technique for each location to help get you jump-started and increase your odds of a successful day's fishing.

As you visit the waters described in this book, perhaps you will find a place or two that draws you back again and again until you eventually become expert at fishing there. And while exploring the locations described in this book, you will inevitably discover other places to cast your line through your own travels or by talking with fellow anglers. That's part of the purpose of this book as well, to start you down the road to discovering the many fishing opportunities much closer to your home than you may have realized.

Barton Park offers excellent access to the Clackamas River for a variety of angling techniques (site 15).

Getting Started

As tempting as it is for the avid angler, raring to get out on the water as soon as possible, to grab his or her gear and head out the door, it's advisable to first consider a few things that will make your fishing trip more enjoyable and safer, and increase the odds of success. First and foremost, you need to be legal. That includes having a current angling license and tags (depending on what species of fish you are out for), and checking the regulations for the waters you intend to fish. Other considerations include the obvious, such as bringing the right gear for the species you want to pursue, as well as the less obvious, including being able to tell wild fish from hatchery fish (important because in some waters wild fish must be released unharmed) or how to guard against spreading invasive species harmful to native aquatic ecosystems. What follows in this chapter is a little advice to get you started.

LICENSES AND REGULATIONS

Managing Oregon's recreational fisheries, with its variety of species, including anadromous fish, and the mix of habitats they occupy, is a complex job and by necessity results in regulations that can be complex as well.

All the waters described in this guide are within the Oregon Department of Fish and Wildlife's Willamette Zone. You will find the regulations for this region of the state described in the *Oregon Sport Fishing Regulations* booklet published every year. As a general rule, lakes and ponds are open all year and streams

An angler still fishes with bait on Henry Hagg Lake near the Elk Picnic Area (site 5).

are open from late May through the end of October. But make sure you double-check the waters listed, as some streams and lakes have special rules, and regulations can change from year to year. If the water you are planning to fish is not specifically listed, the general regulations and bag limits apply.

Oregon has a variety of angling license categories, including resident and nonresident, as well as full season and temporary. Make sure you have one of these before you saunter to water's edge! If you plan to fish for salmon, steelhead, or sturgeon, you will also need a Combined Angling Tag. A couple of interesting options you may want to consider include a Hatchery Harvest Tag, which allows you to catch additional hatchery salmon and

A sturgeon angler waits patiently alongside the Gilbert River for a bite (site 2).

steelhead, and a Two-Rod Angling License that permits anglers to fish with two rods simultaneously.

The Oregon Sport Fishing Regulations booklet is available at many sporting goods stores and Oregon Department of Fish and Wildlife offices, and may be downloaded from the ODFW website at www.dfw.state.or.us.

WATERS OF THE PORTLAND AREA

The places to fish described in this guide include both still water (lakes and ponds) and flowing water (rivers and streams), each of which requires some different fishing techniques and provides different angling experiences. While all the basic angling methods—bait, lures, and flies—can be used on both types of waters, there are some differences in approaches and presentations. For the longtime angler this is pretty basic, but for those with less experience, it is useful to briefly describe some of the differences to help make a decision as to whether you have the necessary equipment and are interested in that kind of fishing.

Lakes and ponds are ideal for still fishing with bait, one of the simplest and most effective angling techniques. As such, it is especially good for beginning anglers and youngsters. The idea is to place bait in the water column where the fish are active. The two approaches here are floating bait beneath a bobber or off the bottom. Fishing with lures such as spinners and spoons generally involves casting and retrieving. Fly fishing is also a perfectly effective still-water angling method. While it is possible to cast dry flies to rising fish, a popular approach is to cast wet flies, such as streamers, then slowly strip line in to simulate a baitfish swimming through the water. Often the increased mobility of having a boat or other floating device gives the angler an advantage over bank-bound fishers.

Fishing in still waters is often best around structures, areas that offer fish places to hide or feed such as around rocks, submerged logs, and stumps or around points. Fish behavior also plays a role in determining the best places and times to fish. For example, some species, such as bass, come close to the shoreline in the spring to spawn. In the heat of the summer, fish are more likely to be found in the deeper parts of a lake where the water is cold. In the winter, fish will congregate closer to the surface.

On the other hand, the moving water of streams and rivers presents a different situation for the angler. Bait fishing with

Kelly Point Park at the mouth of the Willamette River can be a particularly productive location for sturgeon (site 3).

a bobber is certainly possible in moving water, but usually involves letting the bait drift through runs and pools, then reeling in and casting again. This is a technique often used to target salmon and steelhead. Casting and retrieving lures on rivers is similar to the method used in still water, but the angler is usually casting across the current or looking for pools. Fast-moving streams and rivers were made for fly fishing (although in reality, the other way around), and fly anglers let their dry and wet flies be carried in the current or they cast to pools, eddies, and other likely spots.

As with still-water fishing, anglers are also looking for structure in moving water, which is often more obvious than it is in lakes and ponds, where logs and other fish-attracting debris are often hidden beneath the glassy surface. However, the currents found in streams and rivers may make it more challenging for the angler to cast his or her offering in just the right spot.

PORTLAND-AREA GAME FISH

While anglers fishing in the general Portland area will by no means encounter all the fish species Oregon has to offer, there are ample opportunities to catch the state's premier cold-water game fish—salmon and steelhead and trout—along with a full palette of warm-water game fish such as bass, perch, and bluegill. In fact, there are several locations in the Portland metropolitan area where you can catch warm-water fish, a category of game fish that provides lots of enjoyable fishing opportunities and is becoming increasing popular with Oregon anglers.

Following is a basic rundown of the fish species you may catch at the locations described in this book, along with a brief overview of the fishing techniques most commonly used to catch them.

Chinook and Coho Salmon

Many longtime Oregon anglers consider salmon to be the state's signature game fish. Although Oregon has four native species of salmon, Portland-area anglers will mostly encounter chinook and coho. And that's fine, because these two species are generally at the top of the desirability list for most salmon anglers.

Chinook salmon are categorized into two different groups—fall chinook and spring chinook (sometimes spring-summer chinook)—based on the time of year the spawning run begins and the fish start coming inland from the sea. Chinook salmon generally spawn between May and January. The exact timing of the run often varies depending on the river system, but for the lower Columbia and Willamette basins covered in this book, spring chinook runs typically begin in March or April and continue well into the summer. Fall chinook runs tend to occur in August and September.

Chinook salmon fry stay in their natal stream for anywhere from three months to a year or more. Chinook spend two to four years in the ocean before returning to freshwater to spawn. By then the average Oregon-bound chinook has grown to 10 to 30 pounds, with larger ones possible.

Coho salmon only have one seasonal run that typically takes place in November and December, but there is some variability, with runs sometimes starting as early as September. They spawn in smaller streams than do chinook, and their fry spend up to two years in freshwater before migrating to the ocean, where they stay for one or two years before returning to spawn. Oregon coho are typically in the 5- to 10-pound range.

More precise run dates for both species are noted in this book's angling location descriptions where applicable. Oregon has both wild and hatchery runs of salmon, with some protected under the federal Endangered Species Act.

Angling techniques for chinook and coho are similar, with the primary difference being where to fish for them. Trolling with a hook baited with herring is an old favorite for boat-based anglers, along with trolling or back-trolling lures such as Kwikfish and Flatfish plugs. Drifting bait such as shrimp or salmon eggs under a bobber is another tried-and-true technique that can be successful from a boat or shore. Drifting corkies—lures designed to look like a cluster of salmon eggs—is another popular and effective salmon-catching method, as is casting spinners and spoons from a boat or shore. Some anglers fly fish for salmon with baitfish patterns or colorful attractor flies.

Chinook salmon prefer the slower-moving, deeper parts of rivers, and deep holes often provide excellent fishing opportunities for them. On the other hand, coho salmon swim closer to the surface and are not likely to be found in the deeper parts of a river.

Steelhead
Die-hard steelheaders will tell you that this is the king of Oregon's game fish. Although a large number of anglers fish for them with great success using familiar salmon techniques, there is also a dedicated contingent of steelhead fly anglers. For the fly

fisher, Matukas, Marabous, Woolly Buggers, Purple Perils, and Green Butte Skunks are some of the standard offerings.

Steelhead have summer and winter spawning runs, although unlike salmon, they don't necessarily die after spawning. Steelhead fry remain in the stream where they were born for one to four years, then spend a similar period growing to adulthood in the ocean. Rivers where the summer and winter runs overlap may have steelhead in them year-round. Steelhead in Oregon rivers average 5 to 15 pounds.

Areas of relatively shallow, moderately moving water and resting spots are where steelheaders often look to hook one of these prize fish.

Cutthroat and Rainbow Trout

Many streams in the Portland area have native cutthroat trout as well as hatchery rainbow trout. The same holds true for local ponds and lakes, which are often stocked regularly with hatchery rainbows.

Trout can be successfully caught with just about any common fishing technique and gear. That includes bottom fishing with bait, bait floated under a bobber, casting or trolling spinners and spoons, and, of course, fly fishing. Dry flies and nymphs are the favored approaches, with the latter often being more effective for catching larger fish, or when trout are not visibly feeding on the surface.

Shad

An Atlantic Ocean native, American shad were introduced to the Pacific off California in the 1870s and since then have spread

St. Louis Ponds is an especially good place to take kids or beginners fishing, but adults enjoy it also (site 10).

into several Oregon rivers, notably the Columbia, which now has runs of up to two million fish. Shad are, like salmon and steelhead, anadromous. The young fish are born in freshwater and stay there for one to two years before going out to sea to grow to adulthood. They remain at sea for four or five years before returning to spawn in the spring.

Shad offer excellent and popular fishing on the Columbia and Willamette Rivers when the run is in. To catch them, anglers cast a variety of lures, such as small spinners and darts.

White Sturgeon
An ancient line of fish, the bottom-feeding white sturgeon can reach 200 pounds in weight. The Columbia and Willamette

Rivers have good populations of white sturgeon that provide a popular fishery. Anglers fish for them in deep holes and channels using eel, mud shrimp, and smelt for bait, holding it on the bottom with heavy weights. Heavy-duty rod-and-reel outfits with 40- to 60-pound-test lines are needed to haul in these monsters of the deep.

Largemouth and Smallmouth Bass

Bass fishing has become increasingly popular in Oregon in recent years despite the fact that bass are not native to the region. Portland-area anglers are in luck because many lakes, ponds, and rivers offer outstanding opportunities to catch these hard-hitting fish.

Although both are warm-water fish, their habitat preferences differ. Largemouth bass frequent warmer water in lakes and ponds and slower-moving river segments, where they are often found closer to the surface. They also like weedy areas, aquatic vegetation, and underwater structures such as logs, stumps, and rocks. They spawn in the spring and summer and begin moving closer to shore when the water temperature reaches 60°F.

Smallmouth bass prefer slightly colder water temperatures and are less fond of areas with aquatic vegetation. These fish like stretches of river with gravel bottoms, and rocky or sandy-bottom areas in lakes. They are also often found in riffles and eddies in rivers, and off rocky points in lakes.

Most bass anglers use lures, including plastics that imitate frogs, salamanders, and nightcrawlers, as well as jigs, crankbaits, minnow plugs, vibrating plugs, and stickbaits. Many fly anglers go after bass using hairbugs, poppers, and flies tied to resemble mice, minnows, and frogs.

Walleye

Another nonnative fish, walleye offer good angling opportunities in selected sections of the Columbia River, where they frequent deep pools with aquatic vegetation, underwater stumps, and other structure. A dedicated group of walleye anglers fish for them with trolling plugs such as Thundersticks and Rockwalkers or spinner and worm rigs.

Perch, Crappie, and Bluegill

These warm-water panfish are fun to catch and good to eat. Many Portland-area waters host good populations of these fish, which can provide an enjoyable day's fishing. The primary panfish species found in Oregon (although introduced) consist of yellow perch, black crappie, white crappie, and bluegill. They like ponds, lakes, sloughs, and slow-moving rivers. Anglers catch them with worms off the bottom or under a bobber, jigging, and casting small lures such as spinners and spoons.

Catfish and Bullhead

Channel catfish and brown bullhead are found in a number of Portland-area rivers, lakes, and ponds. Although among the less glamorous of Oregon's sport fish, they can provide a fun, laid-back angling experience. You'll find brown bullhead on the sandy bottoms of slow-water areas. Channel catfish prefer clearer water with more current. The best approach to catching these fish is with worms or PowerBait fished off the bottom.

IDENTIFYING WILD FISH AND HATCHERY FISH

Being able to identify the fish you catch is important for a number of reasons. Obviously, you need to know what species of fish you are fishing for and what they look like so you know if you are catching them. In addition, angling rules on some waters may allow you to keep some species but require you to release others depending on the location and season of the year.

Particularly critical is the ability to tell the difference between hatchery-origin fish and wild fish. This is important because in many Oregon waters, particularly in rivers and streams, wild fish often must be released unharmed. This generally applies to salmon, steelhead, and to a lesser extent trout. In the case of salmon and steelhead, some runs may include wild fish that are protected under the federal Endangered Species Act, or the wild fish population is depressed and cannot sustain harvest. The same situation may be true for trout. Trout streams may also be managed as catch-and-release wild fisheries to provide a specific type of angling experience.

Most hatchery fish have their adipose fins clipped before they are released, so anglers can tell the difference by checking to see if their catch's fin is still intact. *The Oregon Sport Fishing Regulations* booklet has good information on fish identification.

CATCH-AND-RELEASE

Equally important to being able to identify your catch is the ability to release the fish unharmed when desired. You may want to do this because you are just out fishing for enjoyment and don't intend to bring your catch home to eat, or it may be a legal requirement. This may be the case in some salmon, steelhead, and trout fisheries where wild fish are protected under the Endangered Species Act and must be released, or it may be a conservation measure if populations are low enough that harvesting them could damage the fishery. In some waters, catch-and-release may be used as a management tool to provide a specific type of angling experience.

To properly release a fish, first wet your hands to prevent damaging its slime covering. After carefully removing the hook from its mouth, cradle the fish in your hand and place it gently in the water with its mouth facing upstream. This allows water to flow though its mouth and gills, providing oxygen to help it revive after its battle. If you are in still water, move the fish back and forth a little to run water through its gills. Take your time to let it gain its energy back before allowing it to slip out of your hand and swim away. Unhooking and releasing the fish without ever removing it from the water is the ideal.

CONSERVATION

Conservation is an integral part of fishing, and all anglers should be as concerned with leaving enough fish for future generations to catch as they are with catching fish themselves. Of particular concern these days is the threat of spreading nonnative, invasive aquatic species that can do significant damage to native fish and the watery ecosystem. Anglers are at the forefront of this battle.

Hydrilla, an aquatic plant; zebra and quagga mussels; mitten crabs; and New Zealand mudsnails top the list of threats to Oregon's fisheries. Cleaning and drying your gear and boat before going back and forth between different bodies of water and knowing what invasive species look like are ways anglers can help prevent their spread.

You can find out more about invasive species at www.clr .pdx.edu.

SAFETY

Water is potentially dangerous, and because that's where the fish live, anglers spend a lot of time around and in it. Be sure to dress properly, with warm clothes and rain gear, and extra clothing in case you get wet. Always wear a life vest when in a boat or other floating device—and a life vest when wading fast, deep, or difficult water is not a bad idea either. A wading staff will also help you keep your balance. And don't forget to tell somebody where you are going and when you expect to return.

RESOURCES

There are several organizations that can provide you with a variety of information on fishing and fish conservation in Oregon. Below are a few of the larger ones. Many smaller fishing organizations and clubs exist as well. You can locate these by contacting the Oregon Department of Fish and Wildlife, asking at your local sporting goods shop, or conducting a Web search.

Oregon Department of Fish and Wildlife (Headquarters)
3406 Cherry Ave. NE
Salem, OR 97303-6000
(503) 947-6000
www.dfw.state.or.us

ODFW Northwest Region Office
17330 SE Evelyn St.
Clackamas, OR 97015
(971) 673-6000

Washington Department of Fish and Wildlife
1111 Washington St. SE
Olympia, WA 98501
(360) 902-2200
www.wdfw.wa.gov

Association of Northwest Steelheaders
P.O. Box 22065
Milwaukie, OR 97269
(503) 653-4176
www.nwsteelheaders.org

Native Fish Society
221 Molalla Ave., Suite 100
Oregon City, OR 97045
(503) 496-0806
www.nativefishsociety.org

Oregon Marine Board
435 Commercial St. NE, #400
Salem, OR 97309-5065
(503) 378-8587
www.boatoregon.com

Oregon Invasive Species Hotline
(866) 468-2337

Oregon State Police Turn In Poachers (TIP) Line
(800) 452-7888

Federation of Fly Fishers
P.O. Box 1688
Livingston, MT 59047
(406) 222-9369
www.fedflyfishers.org

Trout Unlimited
1300 N 17th St., Suite 500
Arlington, VA 22209-2404
(800) 834-2419
www.tu.org

Northwest of Portland

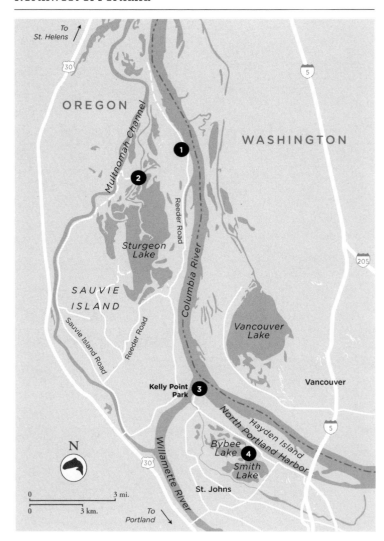

1. Walton Beach, Columbia River, Sauvie Island Wildlife Area

Distance from downtown Portland: 19 miles

Approximate driving time: 40 minutes

Species available: Winter steelhead, spring chinook salmon, sturgeon

Best times to fish: December through March for winter steelhead; late February through June for spring chinook

Best fishing method: Plunking Spin-n-Glos, or bottom fishing with bait

Recommended map: Oregon Department of Fish and Wildlife *Sauvie Island Wildlife Area Map*

Licensing: Oregon Angling License; Sauvie Island Wildlife Area Parking Permit; Combined Angling Tag (for salmon,

Walton Beach, on the Columbia River, is a good place to head when the winter steelhead start running.

steelhead, sturgeon, and halibut); Hatchery Harvest Tag (optional, to catch additional hatchery salmon and steelhead); Two-Rod Angling License (optional, to use two rods at the same time)

Directions: From Portland, drive about 10 miles west on US 30 toward Scappoose. About 2 miles north of Linton, turn right and cross the bridge onto Sauvie Island at the stoplight. Immediately after crossing Multnomah Channel, turn left onto NW Sauvie Island Road. Continue on NW Sauvie Island Road, bearing right at NW Reeder Road. Beginning at about the 9-mile mark from the bridge, there is extensive parking along the road on the left. Access to the Columbia River shoreline is via several stairways that lead over the berm.

Sauvie Island Wildlife Area is managed by the Oregon Department of Fish and Wildlife and requires a daily parking permit, which can be purchased at Sam's Cracker Barrel (15000 NW Sauvie Island Road), Reeder Beach RV Park (26048 NW Reeder Road), Island Cove Cafe (31421 NW Reeder Road), and the Oregon Department of Fish and Wildlife Sauvie Island Wildlife Area headquarters (18330 NW Sauvie Island Road).

The Fishing

Walton Beach is a noted location to catch Columbia River winter-run steelhead, which pass by Sauvie Island each year between December and March. Because the upstream migrating steelhead generally hug the bank in water ranging from 6 to 15 feet deep, these fish are more accessible to bank anglers than in other reaches of the Columbia where the fish travel farther out

Walton Beach, Gilbert River

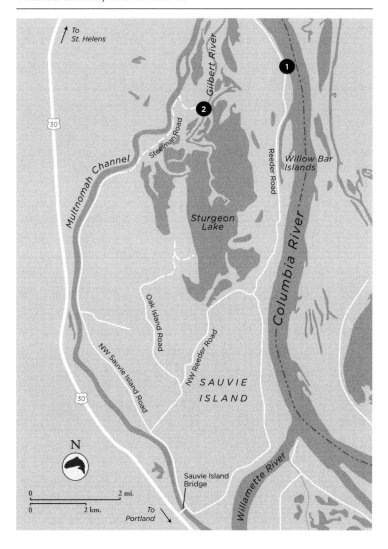

To St. Helens

Gilbert River

Multnomah Channel

Steelman Road

30

Reeder Road

Willow Bar Islands

Sturgeon Lake

Columbia River

Oak Island Road

NW Reeder Road

NW Sauvie Island Road

30

SAUVIE ISLAND

N

0   2 mi.

0   2 km.

Sauvie Island Bridge

To Portland

Willamette River

in the river and are best reached by boat. Beginning at Walton Beach there are several miles of good, open beach access to the river, including Collins Beach, which butts up against Walton Beach to the north.

Although you can cast spinners and spoons to catch steelhead here, plunking is by far the preferred method. Just cast your line out, put it in a rod holder, and wait. The essential strategy for successful plunking is to put your offering in a steelhead travel lane, and since it is known the fish run close to the Sauvie Island shoreline at this location, a cast of 20 yards or less will put you in that lane. Sooner or later a steelhead will come within striking range of your setup and hopefully take it.

Spin-n-Glos are the preferred lure for plunking at Walton Beach. A basic plunking rig involves tying a three-way swivel to the end of your line. A foot-long leader is added to the right-angled swivel, to the end of which a 3- or 4-ounce weight is tied. A 3- to 4-foot leader is then tied to the remaining swivel loop, and the Spin-n-Glo and hook is added to the end of the line. Hook sizes are usually 1/0 to 4/0. Some anglers like to add bait, such as salmon eggs, or some colored yarn to their rig, while others go with the Spin-n-Glo only. Orange and chartreuse are popular colors with Spin-n-Glo anglers. A line weight of 15-pound test or greater is a good idea because it will lessen the chance of breaking off a big fish in the Columbia's strong currents.

This is also an ideal situation to take advantage of the ODFW Two-Rod Angling License and doubling your chances of success. Some anglers tie a bell to their rod tips to indicate when they are getting a hit and which rod is the one requiring attention.

STEELHEAD ON THE MOVE

The steelhead you will catch in the Columbia off Sauvie Island are fish bound for a number of destinations within the Columbia River basin. They're moving upstream to spawn in the streams in which they were born. Some are headed up the Willamette, Deschutes, John Day, or Grande Ronde River basins in Oregon, while others will continue into Idaho and Washington.

Steelhead spawning runs are divided into two groups, winter run and summer run, depending upon when they enter freshwater from the ocean. Winter fish are usually larger when they enter freshwater and spawn sooner than summer-run fish, which may remain in their natal stream for several months before spawning. Winter-run fish are restricted to streams west of the Cascade Range, while steelhead runs east of the Cascades are regarded as summer run, even though you may find them still heading for their spawning grounds in the winter due to the longer distances they must travel. For example, summer-run steelhead are still moving up the Deschutes River in December and January, and don't reach the upper John Day basin until February or March. All steelhead, regardless of whether they are winter or summer run, spawn in the spring and, unlike salmon, don't necessarily die afterward.

This stretch of Sauvie Island shoreline is also a good destination for spring chinook salmon fishing. The timing is perfect because by March, when the winter steelhead fishing is slowing down, the springers are beginning to come through. The run in this section of the river typically happens from late February or March through June.

However, the better location for spring chinook fishing is at Willow Bar, located directly on the Columbia County–Multnomah County line. The Oregon Department of Fish and Wildlife opens the access road specifically for the spring chinook season so anglers can drive out onto the beach. It is not open to motor vehicle access year-round.

To reach Willow Bar from Portland, drive about 10 miles west on US 30 toward Scappoose. About 2 miles north of Linton, turn right and cross the bridge onto Sauvie Island at the stoplight. Immediately after crossing Multnomah Channel, turn left onto NW Sauvie Island Road. Continue on NW Sauvie Island Road, bearing right at NW Reeder Road. Drive about 5 miles, then turn right onto the Willow Bar access road about 0.25 mile past Blue Heron Herbary.

The approach to catching spring chinook here is similar to fishing for winter steelhead a few miles downstream, casting spoons and spinners or plunking, with the latter being the savvy Sauvie Island salmon angler's preferred method.

If you continue down Reeder Road from Walton Beach, north past Collins Beach and the Gilbert River access and boat ramp (where the road becomes gravel) to the end of the road, you will arrive at a favorite location for sturgeon fishing. For sturgeon, you will want to bottom fish with bait such as eel, mud shrimp, and smelt. Line in the 40- to 60-pound-test range and heavy weights up to a pound or more to keep your bait on the bottom is standard rigging for sturgeon fishing in the Columbia River's strong current.

2. Gilbert River, Sauvie Island Wildlife Area

See map on page 5

Distance from downtown Portland: 25 miles

Approximate driving time: 45 minutes

Species available: Sturgeon, largemouth bass, channel catfish, walleye

Best times to fish: Spring and summer

Best fishing method: Casting spoons, spinners and plugs from the bank or still fishing with bait

Recommended map: Oregon Department of Fish and Wildlife *Sauvie Island Wildlife Area Map*

Licensing: Oregon Angling License; Sauvie Island Wildlife Area Parking Permit; Combined Angling Tag (for salmon, steelhead, sturgeon, and halibut); Two-Rod Angling License (optional, to use two rods at the same time)

Directions: From Portland, drive about 10 miles west on US 30 toward Scappoose. About 2 miles north of Linton, turn right and cross the bridge onto Sauvie Island at the stoplight. Immediately after crossing Multnomah Channel, turn left onto NW Sauvie Island Road. Follow NW Sauvie Island Road north for 8.5 miles to where the road becomes gravel. Continue for another 2 miles until the road makes a very sharp right-hand turn. Continue around the turn and go about 0.75 mile until you reach the parking area at Gilbert River.

Sauvie Island Wildlife Area is managed by the Oregon Department of Fish and Wildlife and requires a daily parking permit, which can be purchased at Sam's Cracker Barrel (15000 NW Sauvie Island Road), Reeder Beach RV Park (26048 NW Reeder Road), Island Cove Cafe (31421 NW Reeder Road), and the Oregon Department of Fish and Wildlife Sauvie Island Wildlife Area headquarters (18330 NW Sauvie Island Road).

THE FISHING

This area is closed to the public from October 1 to around April 15 or May 15 each year to protect wintering waterfowl populations. The wildlife area is also a popular duck- and goose-hunting destination during fall and winter. However, since the best fishing opportunities here are in the spring, summer, and early fall, access restrictions really don't affect the angling opportunities.

Sturgeon anglers along the Gilbert River wait patiently for a bite.

The Gilbert River is a warm-water fishery, focusing on sturgeon, channel catfish, largemouth bass, and some walleye. Sturgeon anglers like this location because it's easy to access and offers the deep channels and slower-moving water that sturgeon prefer. These big prehistoric fish stick close to the bottom, and that is where you will want to keep your bait.

There is some discussion among serious sturgeon anglers as to how close to the bottom you should rig your bait, with one camp saying to keep it as near as possible and another insisting that floating as much as several feet from your weight will catch more fish. Whichever way you go, the key is a heavy weight to ensure that your bait stays near the bottom where the sturgeon feed, although the Gilbert River will not require as big a sinker as on the Columbia, with its much stronger current.

A variety of baits are used for sturgeon, but the most reliable standbys are smelt, eel, sand shrimp, and squid. Some sturgeon anglers also use a ball of salmon eggs or pieces of shad and even nightcrawlers. It's not a bad idea to have several different types of bait with you so you can change it out if you are not getting any bites. Believe it or not, sturgeon can be choosy, and some experienced sturgeon anglers say they will avoid bait if it is too dissimilar to what the sturgeon are feeding on naturally at the time. Heavy gear is also a must, including a stout rod-and-reel combination and at least 15- to 30-pound-test line along with large hooks sizes, 5/0 to 9/0.

There is plenty of open bank fishing at and adjacent to the Gilbert River parking lot. Many anglers bring a folding chair, cast their line, and wait for a bite. Look for deeper and slower-moving water to fish. Sturgeon will often nibble awhile at your

AN ANCIENT FISH POPULAR
WITH MODERN ANGLERS

Found on the Pacific coast from Baja California to Alaska (including the Columbia River), white sturgeon have attracted a large contingent of dedicated anglers. The largest freshwater fish in North America, they can grow up to 20 feet long. Sturgeon spawn upstream in the spring and early summer when water temperatures reach 50°F to 64°F. Broadcast spawners, they release their eggs in the water column; the eggs then sink to the river bottom to incubate.

Because of their importance as a recreational fishery, sturgeon are carefully managed by the Oregon Department of Fish and Wildlife, and only those within a specific size range may be taken home to eat. Between 2003 and 2008 recreational anglers caught nearly 180,000 white sturgeon on the lower Columbia River.

bait before biting, so don't try to set the hook too soon. If it looks like you are getting a nibble, wait a bit before reacting. If you don't get any action after a half hour or so, there may be no sturgeon lurking where you have placed your bait, so consider picking up and moving to a different spot for a while.

Make sure you are aware of current sturgeon regulations, as there are strict parameters on the size fish that can be kept. There is also a season quota, and when it is reached in the Gilbert River and adjacent waters, sturgeon fishing will close for the season.

Largemouth bass is another game fish you will encounter on the Gilbert. These fish prefer structure, so you will do better if you walk the banks a little looking for logs, stumps, and other debris that provide shelter. Bass will also feed in more open water near cover where they can retreat if they sense danger, so fishing around and in the vicinity of structure is a good way to find largemouth. Since the location of structure can change from year to year, as logs and other debris are moved around during winter floods, you may have to scout a bit each time you visit. Some structure may be obvious—large logs and stumps sticking out of the water, for example. In other cases, just a few branches poking above the surface may be the only indication of good bass habitat below. In some instances, a small patch of swirling water or irregular current may be your only clue to what lies beneath the surface.

The usual assortment of bass lures will work just fine here. Flashy, colorful spinners such as buzzbaits are a good choice— something that hits the water with a splash and produces a noise when retrieved. Vibrating plugs are good too. Surface lures such as crawlers and chuggers are also a good bet, as well as tried-and-true plastic lures that resemble worms, crayfish, and frogs.

Cast your lure around structure, near the bank, and around brushy areas, but don't ignore open water either. For open water, use the fan technique for more thorough coverage. This is an effective technique used by bass anglers in waters where you can't identify any obvious bass habitat areas. Cast and retrieve your lure in an arc from left to right until you have fished all the water in front of you. Do it one more time, then move on to another piece of water until you have fished the area thoroughly. The more water you cover, the more bass you will catch.

Channel catfish provide for a more relaxed fishing experience. Like sturgeon, they hang out on the river bottom. Fish for them with a weight heavy enough to keep your bait, attached to a short leader, on the bottom. Nightcrawlers and PowerBait are good bets for channel catfish, along with pieces of shad, chicken livers, and crawfish.

Good numbers of walleye can be found in the waters of the lower Columbia River, including the Gilbert River. You can fish for them with worms as well as spinners and spoons, and some anglers even plunk for them. Blue Fox Vibrax and Mepps Aglias are popular spinners. Good walleye spoons include Dardevles and Little Cleos. However, jigs are probably the most commonly used approach. In rivers, walleye are often in the deeper sections.

When casting for walleye, make sure your retrieve is slow enough to take your spinner or spoon nearly to the bottom. If you are casting a jig, let it actually hit the bottom, then lift your rod to bring it off the bottom toward shore. Wait for the jig to fall back to the bottom again, then repeat until you have reeled it in.

If you have a boat, or even a canoe, another option is to put in at the Gilbert boat launch and cruise the river. This will give you better access and allow you to fish more water. To reach the boat ramp, follow NW Sauvie Island Road from US 30, bearing right onto NW Reeder Road. Continue on NW Reeder Road; at about 10 miles, the road will turn to gravel. Continue about 0.9 mile, then turn left at the sign for the Gilbert River boat launch. It is about 0.5 mile to the parking lot, dock, and boat ramp.

3. Willamette and Columbia Rivers, Kelly Point Park

Distance from downtown Portland: 15 miles

Approximate driving time: 25 minutes

Species available: Chinook salmon, steelhead, sturgeon

Best times to fish: Spring and summer for chinook salmon and steelhead; February through October for sturgeon

Best fishing method: Casting spinners and spoons or still fishing from the bank with bait

Recommended map: *Willamette River Recreation Guide*

Licensing: Oregon Angling License Combined Angling Tag (for salmon, steelhead, sturgeon, and halibut); Hatchery Harvest Tag (optional, to catch additional hatchery salmon and steelhead); Two-Rod Angling License (optional, to use two rods at the same time)

Directions: From downtown Portland, travel north on I-405 for 2.5 miles. Take the exit for I-5 and drive on I-5 north for about 4 miles. Get off at exit 307 for Marine Drive. Go left at the exit, then right at the stoplight onto Marine Drive North. Drive 4.2 miles on Marine Drive North, then turn right into Kelly Point Park just before crossing the Columbia Slough. Follow the entrance road about 0.25 mile to the main parking area. From there it is a short walk to the beach along the Columbia River and the mouth of the Willamette River.

The Fishing

The Columbia is a huge river, and it can be an intimidating prospect for anglers confined to its banks and wondering where the best spot to focus on might be. The trick here is to make it manageable, and that means concentrating in and around the mouth of the Willamette River.

River confluences are usually prime fishing locations. Debris washed downstream may collect there, providing good habitat for fish, and food sources are often more abundant as well. Food sources may wash downstream along with debris and out the mouth into the larger river, where swirling currents mix nutrients to create a more fertile environment. Because the Willamette River has healthy runs of spring chinook salmon and steelhead, the mouth is an excellent place to get first crack at them. As a tributary of the Columbia River, the Willamette may also have cooler water flowing from it as opposed to the main stem. If so, upstream-bound Columbia River salmon and steelhead may linger and rest awhile around the river's mouth before continuing their journey, offering anglers a chance to catch them.

Spring chinook run from March through June in this section of the river, where you will encounter both hatchery and wild fish. Only hatchery fish, indicated by a clipped adipose fin, may be kept. The two most often used approaches to catching chinook salmon off the bank at the Willamette's mouth entail casting and retrieving a variety of lures or bait, with plunking the favored method.

Casting for salmon with spinners and spoons is an effective, all-around technique, especially in larger-river situations

Kelly Point Park at the mouth of the Willamette River can be a particularly productive location for sturgeon.

where you need to cover a lot of water and then go back and cover it again in an efficient manner. The more water you fish, and the longer your lure stays in the water, the more fish you will catch. There is no "secret" lure that guarantees success, but determining a color and style the fish will like that particular day often makes a big difference in how well you do. Lures made by Uncle Bud, Blue Fox, Mepps, and Luhr-Jensen are all popular and work equally well. Number 2 and 3 sizes are good choices for large fish like salmon. Having a good selection of spinners and spoons in different colors in your tackle box helps greatly because you can try different lures throughout the day and, by trial and error, hopefully find one

COUNTING COLUMBIA RIVER FISH

Government agencies keep track of the numbers of salmon, steelhead, and other fish that migrate over Bonneville Dam through the fish ladders, located about 40 miles upstream from Kelly Point Park. While this data is collected for purposes of managing fish populations and determining how well the various runs of anadromous fish are faring from year to year, the information is also extremely useful to anglers. You can get a pretty good idea of the best times to get your gear out and head for the river by keeping an eye on the daily tallies of adult fish passing over the dam. When numbers rise, more fish are moving upstream and therefore providing greater opportunities to catch one.

As a rule of thumb, most adult chinook salmon are counted at Bonneville Dam during April and May, and August and September; coho salmon, August through October; steelhead, July through September; and shad, May and June. You can find fish-count information about the Columbia and other Oregon rivers through the Fishing Resources page on the Oregon Department of Fish and Wildlife's website at www.dfw.state.or.us.

that is most effective. Lures consisting of contrasting colored material often work very well.

The sandy, open beach at and near the Willamette's mouth at Kelly Point Park offers plenty of room for casting spinners and spoons. For spoons, cast straight across the river's mouth or slightly upstream, and let the spoon sink briefly before reeling in. Generally, a slower retrieve works better than a rapid one. Fish your spinners by casting either upstream, straight across (as with spoons), or downstream into the Columbia River. With the upstream cast, let the spoon or spinner sink a little. The idea is to get your lure near the river bottom, but not actually dragging or bouncing on the bottom. Keep in mind while fishing for chinook that this species prefers to swim a little deeper than steelhead. Once you have covered all the water at the mouth, move along the beach upstream and spend some time casting into the main-stem Columbia, since the salmon will be moving up this river as well as into the Willamette.

Another creative approach that works well here, especially on the Columbia reach where the current is a little faster, is plunking with a Kwikfish. A Kwikfish is a very popular plug for chinook salmon that is usually trolled, back-trolled, or back-bounced from a boat—techniques that can't be used by a bank angler. However, you can plunk from shore with them. To do that, put a swivel on the end of your line, then add a "dropper" line of about 20 to 30 inches with a 1- to 8-ounce weight. Then add a 48- to 60-inch leader (40- to 60-pound test) to the swivel and attach the Kwikfish to the end of the leader. To make the whole setup more attractive to a salmon, wrap a piece of herring around the middle of the lure with monofilament line. Now, cast the whole rig out into the river and let it do its job. The weight will hold the setup in place while the Kwikfish floats and bounces in the current, acting much like it does when trolled or back-bounced.

Because this method is a more stationary technique than casting lures, it relies on fish passing by the rig and striking the wobbling Kwikfish. For that reason, placing it near the mouth of the Willamette when salmon are moving upstream will give you the best results. The more traditional plunking with bait is also an effective technique, done as described above but using prawns, sand shrimp, or salmon eggs instead of a Kwikfish.

This is also a good location to target steelhead, with the fish moving though here from May through August. You can use the same techniques for steelhead as for salmon, but remember that steelhead tend to swim closer to the surface than do chinook.

Kelly Point Park is also a favorite spot for sturgeon anglers. Sturgeon are in the river year-round, though February through October is generally the best period. Fish for them with a sturdy rod and frozen or fresh smelt, sand shrimp, eel, and herring for bait, held on the bottom with a heavy weight. The best location for sturgeon fishing is right at the Willamette River mouth.

4. Smith and Bybee Lakes

Distance from downtown Portland: 12 miles

Approximate driving time: 20 minutes

Species available: Largemouth bass, crappie, bluegill, yellow perch, brown bullhead

Best times to fish: Late spring through summer

Best fishing method: Casting spinners and plugs or still fishing from the bank or a small watercraft

Recommended map: *AAA Portland Map*

Licensing: Oregon Angling License

Directions: From downtown Portland, travel north on I-405 for 2.5 miles. Take the exit for I-5 and drive on I-5 north for about 4 miles. Get off at exit 307 for Marine Drive. Go left at the exit, then right at the stoplight onto Marine Drive North. Travel 2.1 miles on Marine Drive North, then turn left onto the short access road paralleling Marine Drive at the brown sign for the lakes. There is a parking area with restrooms, and additional parking areas along the access road. A couple short trails lead to Bybee Lake. One is near the parking area and restrooms, and the other is shortly beyond, just before the barricade across the access road.

THE FISHING

Smith and Bybee Lakes are part of a 2,000-acre series of wetlands in the Portland metropolitan area near the confluence of the Willamette and Columbia Rivers. Known officially as the Smith and Bybee Wetlands, and under the management

Located within the Portland metropolitan area, Smith and Bybee Lakes harbor a variety of warm-water fish species.

of Portland Metro Parks, Smith and Bybee are the largest of a number of lakes within the wetland area, with Smith Lake being the larger of the two at about 200 acres. Both lakes offer very nice angling opportunities for a number of warm-water fish species, including largemouth bass, crappie, bluegill, yellow perch, and brown bullhead.

The lakes can be fished either from the bank or by small watercraft such as a canoe or kayak. There is a relatively new canoe launch site accessed by the trail leading from the main parking area, but you can also easily carry and launch a canoe from the undeveloped dirt path near the terminus of the access road. Fishing from a watercraft is preferred here, as you will be able to access more water and more easily avoid areas choked with aquatic vegetation.

Especially important here is to avoid getting your line and lure tangled in aquatic slop, as these lakes can grow a lot of near-shore aquatic vegetation, especially by mid- to late summer, which is the peak growth period for water plants. Weedy areas are generally good for the warm-water species you will find at Smith and Bybee Lakes, especially bass, but very dense aquatic vegetation can be a problem to fish. If you are bank fishing, you may need to walk around the shore of Smith Lake from the access trails off Marine Drive until you find a location with open water and shoreline vegetation not too tangled and overgrown to impair casting. For that reason, wearing rugged clothing that will protect you while walking through brush and briars is a good idea. A pair of low rubber boots or other waterproof footwear will make it easier to traverse muddy and wet shoreline areas.

Warnings about aquatic vegetation notwithstanding, if you are targeting the lakes' largemouth bass, don't ignore the weedy areas altogether. You want to work the weedy areas and along the margins, but you don't want to try fishing areas so choked with vegetation that your lure gets hung up or covered in goop. And even cover-loving fish such as bass have their limits.

Being warm-water fish, angling for largemouth bass tends to be slow here during the winter months. Bass fishing begins to pick up in the spring when the water temperature gets to 60°F. The bass are then coming closer to shore to spawn and looking for food, making them more accessible and easier to find than in the open water in the middle of the lakes. It is therefore important to keep an eye on the spring weather and warming trends. Bass up to 4 pounds have been caught here.

Start by exploring areas of cover with a fast-moving surface lure that will attract actively feeding bass. Consider starting with spinner baits. Widely used by expert bass anglers, their bent shaft design keeps them from getting hung up in the weeds and brush. Spinner baits are also commonly used to feel out where the bass are by arousing their interest. If it turns out that the bass are reacting to the spinner bait but not striking, at least you know where the fish are and you can start presenting them with other kinds of lures until you find the "hot" one for the day. One-quarter to 1-ounce weights are the best spinner bait sizes for largemouth bass. It's good to have a number of styles and colors on hand as well.

Begin by casting your spinner bait around and in (if the weeds aren't too dense) areas of aquatic cover, including vegetation, sunken brush, and logs. Retrieve the lure briskly at first to make it ride at or just above the surface. This will create a disturbance that may attract any bass in the area, even if they are not inclined to bite it. But stay alert—strikes on spinner baits are often low-key and easily missed. If you detect a tug, even a subtle one, set the hook. If the fast retrieve isn't producing any results, slow down a little so the lure runs below the surface. If you have a good "feel," you can slow your retrieve down enough to make it hop on the bottom.

If you're still not getting anywhere, cast a plastic worm and let it sink a bit before reeling it in, then repeat. Cover as much of the area that looks "bassy" as you can. Another trick is to put a little bit of nightcrawler or pork strip on the hook of a spinner bait.

WARM-WATER FISH,
LATECOMERS TO OREGON'S ANGLING SCENE

Oregon only has one native warm-water game fish, the Lost River sucker, also known as mullet, which is now protected under the Endangered Species Act. Largemouth bass were introduced to Oregon's Willamette River in the 1880s, and by the mid-1890s black and white crappie, channel catfish, and bluegill had also been planted in the Willamette. Striped bass, a native of the Atlantic coast, became established in some Oregon rivers, most notably the Columbia, by the early part of the twentieth century. Smallmouth bass were introduced into Oregon at Lake Oswego in 1923. Since that time, many of these non-native species have spread to other parts of the state either naturally or deliberately introduced to provide additional fishing opportunities. Other introduced warm-water game fish now found in Oregon include yellow perch, walleye, and American shad.

This can really increase its attraction to bass that are initially reluctant to strike.

If you have a small watercraft, you will be at an advantage since you will be able to work more of the weedy areas, including from the open-water side that is not accessible to bank anglers. You can also access Smith Lake through the connecting slough more easily by boat.

Don't ignore the open water either, as bass are out there as well. You can paddle around to different reaches of open water in a boat, or walk the shorelines and stop at open-water areas. In open water, experienced bass anglers often use the fan technique, which entails casting in a fan pattern from left to right until you have thoroughly fished all the water in front of you. Do this a couple of times, and if nothing is happening, move on to another open-water section.

Any of the standard largemouth bass plugs should work here, such as stickbaits, prop baits, crawlers, and chuggers. Plugs for largemouth bass should range from 2 to 6 inches long.

Many of the techniques used for largemouth bass can be applied to bluegill and yellow perch as well. These fish generally like the same kinds of cover as do bass, but smaller spinners and spoons are the preferred lures. Just about any of the many types of manufactured ones will do.

Crappie tend to be more cautious of surface noises than bass and other species of panfish, so quiet is more the rule when fishing for them. Some of the best fishing for crappie is in early spring, when the water temperatures get into the high 50s and low 60s and the fish come in closer to shore to feed. Although they are found in areas of aquatic vegetation, they are more common in clear water. Small spinners are probably the most effective type of crappie lure. Use brighter-colored or flashier spinners if the water seems a little murky. Crappie also tend to swim in schools, so if you start getting hits, keep fishing in that location. If the bite falls off because the school has moved on, wait awhile because they sometimes will come back.

There are also brown bullhead in the lakes. These are most effectively caught with bait such as nightcrawlers or PowerBait fished off the bottom.

Southwest of Portland

Southwest of Portland

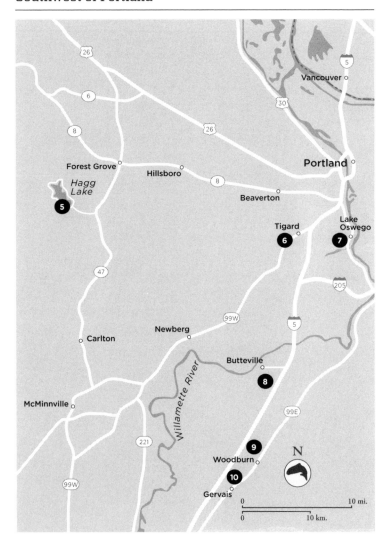

5. Henry Hagg Lake, Scoggins Valley Park

Distance from downtown Portland: 37 miles

Approximate driving time: 1 hour

Species available: Rainbow and cutthroat trout, smallmouth bass, crappie, perch, catfish

Best times to fish: Spring through fall

Best fishing method: Casting spinners, spoons, and plastics or bait from the bank

Recommended maps: Oregon road map, *Gaston USGS Quad Topo Map*

Licensing: Oregon Angling License, Daily Park Pass

Directions: From Portland, drive west on US 26 for about 5 miles and take exit 2A to Highway 217. Follow Highway 217 toward Beaverton and Tigard for about 3 miles. Turn right onto Highway 8 toward Beaverton and go west for about 15 miles to Forest Grove. At Forest Grove go south on Highway 47 for 9.5 miles and turn right onto SW Scoggins Valley Road at the sign for Scoggins Valley Park/Hagg Lake. Follow SW Scoggins Valley Road for 3.2 miles and turn left onto SW Shore Lane at the sign for Boat Ramp/Recreation Area C. Go about 0.5 mile, crossing over the dam, to the Elk Picnic Area on the right.

There is a day-use fee and a boat-pass fee if you intend to launch a boat. A fee booth is located at the park entrance and includes a self-service station if park staff is not on duty when you arrive.

THE FISHING

The 1,100-acre Henry Hagg Lake, used for water storage and flood control, is located within Washington County's Scoggins Valley Park and provides excellent and easily accessible fishing opportunities for trout and a number of warm-water fish species. The lake is normally closed to the public from late November to early March, so this is a spring through fall fishery.

Although there are some native cutthroat trout here, the lake is heavily stocked with rainbow trout by the Oregon Department of Fish and Wildlife, so these hatchery fish provide the bulk of the trout-fishing opportunities. Hatchery fish planted in the lake the previous spring that survive the winter can reach up to 6 pounds by the following year. Most of the stocked trout are released near the dam, where the water is deeper, making the south end of the lake a good area to concentrate your fishing efforts.

You can fish right at the base of the dam by walking down the riprap from the Elk Picnic Area. There are many good areas to fish from the bank immediately below the picnic area, including some points that become more prominent when the water level has dropped, especially in the fall. At very low pool, when the water is too shallow around the picnic area, you can drive north along the lake's west shoreline to Recreation Area C, where there is good bank-fishing access. The long fishing pier located there is also a good place to fish if you have younger kids along. There is also a boat ramp here, as well as at several other locations along the lake, but you do not need a boat to have productive fishing at Hagg Lake.

Just about any standard fishing technique will work for Hagg Lake trout, but small spinners, including Mepps Aglias, Rooster

Points are an excellent place to fish on Henry Hagg Lake during the fall when water levels are lower.

Tails, and Blue Fox Vibrax, are some of the favorites. Small spoons are also good. Use larger, more colorful or flashier lures in the early spring, when the water is cooler, and on cloudy days and early in the morning and evening, when there is less light. When the water is warmer or the skies are brighter, go with the opposite—smaller, darker-colored lures. The idea is that fish are more sluggish in colder water so the larger, flashier lures are needed to motivate them to strike. When the light is murky, the fish are also better able to see bigger, more colorful offerings. In warmer water and bright light, smaller lures and more subtle colors are less likely to spook the fish. As a general guideline, slower retrieves are usually better than fast retrieves for catching fish, but varying the speed of your retrieve to help make your lure act more like the baitfish it is designed to imitate can up the odds of a strike.

Fishing with bait is an equally popular technique for Hagg Lake trout, with worms, PowerBait, corn, marshmallows, and salmon eggs being the typical offerings. Floating bait under a bobber is the basic tried-and-true bait-fishing method, and is especially good for kids since it's obvious when you are getting a bite. Add a little bit of weight if you are using marshmallows or PowerBait to get it to sink more quickly.

A more sophisticated approach to bait fishing is plunking, where you float your bait in the water column above the lake bottom. As your bait sways in the underwater currents, its movement will help attract fish. This is a good way to go on bright, sunny days when fish are holding closer to the bottom to avoid being seen by predators such as osprey. Attach a weight 18 to 20 inches below your hook. Bait the hook with a worm, then add PowerBait or a small marshmallow around the eye of the hook. This will keep your bait floating above the weight as it rests on the lake bottom. You can vary the distance between the weight and the hook depending on where you want to float your bait in the water column.

Although there are some largemouth bass in Henry Hagg Lake, it is known more for its ample smallmouth bass population, which includes trophy-size fish. The state's record smallmouth bass was caught here in 2005.

Early to mid-spring is the best time to target smallmouth bass as they move into shallow areas along the lake to spawn. There are some small coves and irregularities along the southern shoreline that are worth exploring, though you are better

A LAKE OF RECORD

Henry Hagg Lake is notable in that it has produced two of Oregon's record-size warm-water game fish. In 2005 angler Nick Rubeo caught an 8-pound, 1.76-ounce smallmouth bass here, and in 2001 Bob Judkins landed a 3-pound, 7-ounce bullhead catfish. As of this writing, both those records still hold.

Only one other Oregon water has produced as many record warm-water fish as Hagg Lake. In 1991 an 11-ounce green sunfish was caught in the Umpqua River, and in 1973 angler Beryl Bliss hauled a monster 68-pound striped bass out of the river. That striped bass remains Oregon's largest of that species, and the largest warm-water fish, caught to date. Next in line is a flathead catfish caught on the Snake River in 1994 that weighed in at 42 pounds. The third-largest warm-water fish on record is a 36-pound, 8-ounce channel catfish caught in McKay Reservoir in eastern Oregon in 1980. The smallest record-size warm-water fish currently recorded is a 7.68-ounce pumpkinseed sunfish caught in Lake Oswego in 1996.

off driving the road around the lake and fishing the inlets of the various arms, including Sain Creek and Scoggins Creek on the west shore and Tanner Creek on the east shore. However, as summer comes on and the water warms, the bass tend to move into the cooler, deeper water on the south end of the lake, especially around the dam, where you can fish for them off the riprap just below SW Shore Lane as it crosses the dam.

When fishing for bass in the morning or evening, use surface plugs such as stickbaits, or spinners, including standards such as Rooster Tails, along with spinner baits and buzzbaits. Retrieve your spinner bait fast enough for it to stay near or even break the surface. Switch to subsurface lures during the afternoon, when the bass are staying deeper to avoid predators. Good choices include crankbaits, minnow plugs, and vibrating plugs. Plastic lures are also good for midday fishing—especially ones molded to look like crayfish or worms.

To target perch and crappie, walk around the shoreline and look for areas with aquatic weed growth or other underwater structure. This is the type of habitat in which these species like to hide and feed. Small spinners, bait under a bobber, and plunking are all effective for perch. Bait-and-bobber works very well for perch during the summer months here.

For crappie, a bobber and jig setup is the preferred Hagg Lake rig, but small spinners will work too. Tie a jig to the end of your line below the bobber—you can utilize a dropper to attach a second jig if you want—and vary the distance between jig and bobber until you find the most effective combination, meaning the right depth for where the crappie are holding. Cast the rig out into the lake, let it sit for a moment, then reel it in a little somewhat abruptly, let it sit for a moment, and then repeat until you have reeled it ashore. Set the hook as soon as you feel a bite, or the fish may spit it out without hooking itself.

Some catfish are also in the lake, and they are usually caught by fishing bait off the bottom.

6. Tualatin River, Cook Park

Distance from downtown Portland: 12 miles

Approximate driving time: 25 minutes

Species available: Largemouth bass, crappie, bluegill, channel catfish

Best times to fish: Spring and summer

Best fishing method: Casting flies, spinners, spoons, plugs, and plastics from a small boat, kayak, canoe, pontoon boat, or float tube

Recommended map: Oregon road map

Licensing: Oregon Angling License

Directions: Cook Park is located in Tigard. To reach it, take I-5 south and get off at exit 291 about 8 miles from downtown Portland. At the stop sign turn east onto SW Upper Boones Ferry Road and drive 0.2 mile to a stoplight. Turn left to stay on SW Upper Boones Ferry Road for another 0.2 mile, then turn right onto SW Durham Road. Follow SW Durham Road for 0.9 mile, turning left onto SW 92nd Avenue. You will enter the park 0.5 mile down this road. Continue past the playing fields for 0.4 mile to reach the parking area and boat ramp along the river.

The Fishing

Don't let this reach of the Tualatin River fool you. Although the current here is almost imperceptible and the river can sometimes be a bit turbid as well, it offers nice warm-water angling opportunities for largemouth bass, crappie, bluegill, and even some channel catfish.

Cook Park is a great place to launch a small watercraft and fish for bass and other warm-water species.

While there is a small beach and boat dock from which you can fish from shore, this portion of the Tualatin River is almost custom-made for fishing from a small craft. In the slow-moving current, pontoon boats work great. A canoe or kayak is another ideal choice and allows anglers to paddle up and down along the brushy bank, alternately casting into mid-river and river margins. Despite the stream's narrow channel, even a small boat with an electric or small gasoline motor will fill the bill.

Most craft angling is done from about 0.25 mile in either direction from the boat dock. Venturing farther upstream or downstream increases the risk of encountering debris dams deposited during previous high-flow periods, along with the dangers they pose to boaters. Except for the small beach found at the boat put-in, the banks of the river are steep and choked with vegetation, making angling access virtually impossible anywhere else in the park. At this location having some kind of floating craft will significantly improve your success rate.

Largemouth bass is probably the most desirable of the species found in the Tualatin River, and offers some pretty good opportunities. Largemouth in Oregon average 2 to 5 pounds, and that is around what you might catch here.

For starters, largemouth bass are more active in low-light conditions, so planning your fishing trip to Cook Park for early morning, late afternoon, early evening, or overcast days will make a difference. Fishing for largemouth is best here beginning in the spring, as water temperatures rise, and lasts through the summer, until the cooling autumn rains begin to fall. Due to water temperature, the bass will tend to hang out closer to the surface, generally within 10 feet or so. Largemouth become

THE CHALLENGE OF KEEPING CLEAN WATER
FLOWING IN URBAN FISHERIES

Much of the lower Tualatin River flows through a suburban and urban environment, and that presents a serious challenge when it comes to keeping the river clean enough to provide good fishing opportunities. The most pressing problem involves pollutants washed into the stream during rainstorms, a common situation in the Tualatin River basin. These pollutants can range from sediment that may smother fish eggs to oil, fertilizers, pesticides, industrial chemicals, and soap from washing vehicles. Many of these chemicals are known to be toxic to fish.

Effectively addressing urban stream pollution is very difficult because it originates from so many different sources and locations. Regulations can help, but public education is equally important. Learn how to reduce the use of chemicals that might end up in local streams and rivers such as cutting down on your use of fertilizers and insecticides and buying biodegradable soaps and similar products.

more active in the spring as spawning season approaches and water temperatures reach 60°F. The bite will start to drop off as water temperatures dip to 50°F and below.

Bass also like cover provided by vegetation and structure, defined as anything that changes the configuration of the riverbed, including rocks and sunken logs, stumps, and root wads. While the Tualatin River definitely has underwater structure, the nature of the water can make it difficult to see unless you can detect telltale surface currents, or a bit of a branch poking out of the water. Your best bet is to paddle up and down the river while casting your lure toward the brushy edges, and around logs and other structures if you can find clues to identify their location in the main current. This will help cover all your bases, as bass like to hang out in shallower, warmer water but close to cover and structure.

Murkier water actually has some advantages for largemouth fishing in that the bass won't see you as readily as in clearer water and therefore are less easily spooked. It also makes your offerings less visible to the fish, and that needs to be taken into consideration. In these kinds of water conditions, bass rely more on their lateral line, which detects vibrations in the water, so vibrating lures are a big advantage when fishing at Cook Park. However, the bass will still use sight to find and catch food, making flashy and more colorful lures a good idea here as well.

Spinners are good overall lures to use here for bass—the flashier and more colorful the better. Even better are buzzbaits, which are spinners that make a good splash when they hit the water and a gurgling noise as they're retrieved. That noisy presentation helps get the attention of hungry bass in water with low visibility, and works particularly well in the Tualatin River's very lazy current. Reel them in fairly quickly, with enough speed to keep the lure half in and half out of the water for maximum effectiveness.

A variety of plugs will also work well here. Vibrating plugs are a good choice, as well as crawlers and chuggers, both of which produce noises as they are reeled in that are attractive to bass. Vibrating plugs are generally sinkers, while crawlers and chuggers are surface lures. You'll want plugs that are 2 to 6 inches long for largemouth bass.

Brightly colored plastic worms are also proven largemouth bass getters. Cast the worm out and keep the line tight as it sinks, because that is typically when you will get a strike. Too much slack and you won't feel the strike in time to set the hook. Fish worms as you would the other bass lures, casting toward the brushy bank and where you think there is underwater structure, but don't limit yourself. The more water you cover, the more bass you will likely catch.

This river reach also holds crappie and bluegill, both fun species to catch, with habitat preferences and fishing techniques similar to largemouth bass. Follow the same approach as for largemouth, but use small spinners and spoons. Flashy and colorful is better when water visibility is low.

If you don't have access to a watercraft, you can still fish for largemouths, although you will be limited to the beach and dock area. To efficiently cover the most water, try the fan technique that serious bass anglers use when fishing smaller, featureless waters. Cast and retrieve your lure in an arc from left to right until you have fished all the water in front of you. Do it a second time, then move up- or downstream a little to cover another stretch of water until you have fished the entire beach area. This method will actually keep you and your lure busy for quite a while before you run out of water. You can fish for crappie and bluegill from the shore as well, but it isn't necessary to be so methodical, and casting and retrieving spinners and spoons in a more random pattern will do just fine.

There is also always the option of catching channel catfish, which like to hang out on the river bottom and lend themselves to old-fashioned still fishing with bait from the bank. You can catch these fish with nightcrawlers or PowerBait fished off the bottom.

7. Willamette River, George Rogers Park

Distance from downtown Portland: 8.5 miles

Approximate driving time: 20 minutes

Species available: Chinook salmon, coho salmon, steelhead, largemouth bass, crappie

Best times to fish: March through June for chinook; September for coho; year-round for steelhead; summer for bass and crappie

Best fishing method: Casting spinners, spoons and corkies and plunking with Spin-n-Glos from the bank

Recommended map: *AAA Portland Map*

Licensing: Oregon Angling License; Combined Angling Tag (for salmon, steelhead, sturgeon, and halibut); Hatchery Harvest Tag (optional, to catch additional hatchery salmon and steelhead); Two-Rod Angling License (optional, to use two rods at the same time)

Directions: From downtown Portland, drive south on Highway 43 for about 7 miles. Highway 43 is called South State Street through Lake Oswego. About 0.5 mile south of Lake Oswego center, turn left onto Green Street and follow the road about 0.3 mile to the park and parking area. The beach access area is at the bottom of a set of stairs descending to where the outlet from Lake Oswego flows into the Willamette River.

THE FISHING

George Rogers Park in Lake Oswego offers a good-size beach to fish for Oregon's signature anadromous fish as well as fun-to-catch

George Rogers Park

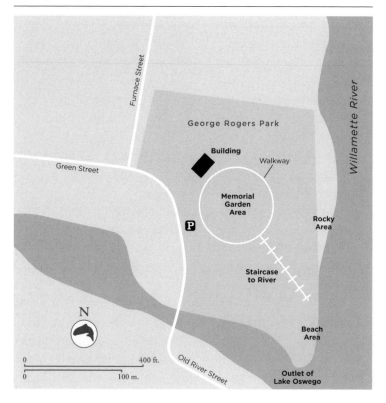

warm-water species. The Willamette River's spring chinook salmon run is an immensely popular fishery. On this reach of the river, the run goes from March through June. Most anglers target this premier game fish from a boat, but bank-bound anglers have a fighting chance to catch them from a number of locations in the general Portland area, and George Rogers Park is one of them. ·

Casting spinners and spoons from the beach is the simplest, most direct approach. It is an effective method, and probably one of the most used. A variety of spinners work well for salmon on the Willamette River, and it often boils down to personal choice. Some spinners favored by salmon anglers include Blue Fox Vibrax and Mepps in sizes 3 and 4. Good colors for chinook include red and orange as well as brass and silver. If the water is turbid, go with brighter colors such as red, yellow, green, and gold. The same goes for spoons: You want good water action and flashes of color to attract a strike. Dick Nites and Little

This public park allows anglers to access the Willamette River to fish for salmon and bass.

SPRING-RUN CHINOOK

The Willamette River spring chinook salmon run is one of the most popular and exciting fisheries in Oregon, and many anglers impatiently endure the early winter months waiting for reports of the first fish to arrive. Typically the Willamette fish begin entering the river between January and April, reaching Willamette Falls at Oregon City between April and August. They spawn in the headwaters of larger streams between August and October, where the next generation of fish remains for a year or so before heading back out to sea. After migrating north as far as southeast Alaska, the salmon return to the Willamette after four to five years to spawn.

The spring chinook run ranges from 50,000 to 100,000 fish each year, though some of those are wild fish protected under the Endangered Species Act and must be released unharmed if caught. Nevertheless, the spring chinook run on the Willamette River offers top salmon-angling opportunities, with fish averaging 10 to 15 pounds and the potential to catch one as big as 40 pounds.

Cleos are a couple of favorites. Make sure you have a variety of colors and styles of both spinners and spoons in your tackle box. If the bite is slow, you can sometimes change that by trying different lures.

When casting your spinner or spoon, throw it either in a straight line across the river as if you are trying to reach the opposite shore, or at a 45-degree angle upstream. Then pause and let the lure sink for a bit. Since chinook usually swim deeper in the water column than other salmon species, the trick is to avoid getting snagged on the bottom. After letting your lure sink for a bit, begin reeling it in, but not too fast. A common mistake spinner and spoon anglers make is retrieving the lure too quickly. A slow, steady pace is usually best, allowing your line and lure to swing at an angle downstream. The strike often comes as the line swings around to its farthest point. Ideally, you will be able to feel the "wobble" in your lure, indicating that it is working properly. If your spinner feels like it's not moving, try giving it a few sharp jerks to reset the blade. That often gets the lure's action moving again.

Drifting corkies and plunking Spin-n-Glos are also good methods to use when bank fishing for salmon on the Willamette. A corkie is basically a lure that resembles a clutch of salmon eggs that you drift with a little weight added, casting the rig into the river, letting it drift by, then casting again. Instead of a corkie, you can also try floating a jig under a bobber. Spin-n-Glos are brightly colored lures with spinner blades that vibrate in the water. A lead weight keeps the setup anchored to the bottom, while the Spin-n-Glo and hook rig is tied off of a swivel on a 30-inch or so leader. Toss it out into the river, let it sit, and wait for a chinook to pass by and take a swipe at it. This is a favored and very effective bank-fishing technique for salmon.

The Willamette River also has an improving coho salmon fishery. The run passes by the George Rogers Park segment in September. Spinners and spoons tend to be the favorite approach for coho angling. The summer steelhead run goes from May until the end of August, while the winter run stretches from

November through March. Chinook salmon techniques also work well for this Oregon game fish.

This is also a good location for some fun summer warm-water angling—bass and crappie in particular. Use small spinners and spoons for the crappie. A slower-paced, more relaxing technique is plain, ol' still fishing with bait, usually worms or PowerBait fished off the bottom with a lead weight.

For bass, spinners are a good bet, but try some of the more specialized types made specifically for bass. Buzzbaits splash loudly when cast into the water and emit a gurgling sound when they are retrieved, which helps entice bass into striking. Vibrating plugs are also good for bass. Or you can fish with the old bass standby, plastic worms. Cast the worm out into the river then let it sink, keeping the line tight so you can detect a strike.

Also work the area where the outlet from Lake Oswego enters the main river, as there is movement of warm-water fish between the two.

8. Wilsonville Pond, Wilsonville

Distance from downtown Portland: 20 miles
Approximate driving time: 30 minutes
Species available: Largemouth bass, bluegill, brown bullhead
Best times to fish: Spring and summer
Best fishing method: Casting streamer flies, spinners, plugs, poppers and plastic worms from the bank or a float tube and still fishing with nightcrawlers
Recommended map: Oregon road map
Licensing: Oregon Angling License

Directions: From Portland, go south on I-5 for about 18 miles and take exit 282. Turn right onto Butteville Road and follow it for 0.1 mile. Bear left onto Boones Ferry Road and stay on it for 1.7 miles. The pond and small parking area is on the west side of the road adjacent to I-5, just past a sharp right curve on Boones Ferry Road. There is a small sign that says Wilsonville Pond at the parking area. The pond is located immediately west of the parking lot.

THE FISHING

Small ponds can offer uncomplicated fishing, and Wilsonville Pond is no exception. It's easy to get to, and at 6 acres is both big enough for an adult to find a good day's fishing and small enough to be manageable for kids and beginning anglers.

Wilsonville Pond offers fishing for largemouth bass, bluegill, and brown bullhead, making it a place that both lure and bait anglers will find worth checking out. The pond's shoreline

WILLAMETTE VALLEY FISHING PONDS

Wilsonville Pond is one of many small ponds scattered throughout the farm and rural communities of the Willamette Valley. Some are natural ponds created when streams became constricted due to geological forces, or are the remnants of old river meanders. Others are farm ponds created to provide water for irrigation or livestock. Still others were developed as log ponds at lumber mill sites. Today, many of these old ponds serve as community fishing destinations and are especially popular with families due to their ease of access. Most have warm-water species, but many are also stocked with rainbow trout by the Oregon Department of Fish and Wildlife. Ponds with natural outlets to the Willamette River or its major tributaries may also have some native cutthroat trout that wander upstream.

is fairly brushy and tree-lined, but a trail that circles it will lead you to a number of open areas where you can swing your line. For better access, especially if you are in search of largemouth bass, a float tube is ideal.

Largemouth bass are probably the most sought-after fish in Wilsonville Pond, and while you can certainly catch them from shore, having a float tube will give you access to much more of the pond's bass habitat. As is typical with bass, they are fairly lethargic during the winter months, becoming livelier and more accessible to the angler as spring comes on and the water becomes warmer. When water temperatures reach

60°F, the bass will become more active, stay closer to the surface, and move in closer to shore, especially to spawn. Once water temperatures drop to 50°F and lower, largemouth bass fishing will drop off as well.

Colorful spinners, plugs, and plastics are the mainstay lures for largemouth fishing, and they will work here as well as they do in any other bass water. Buzzbaits are a good choice. These are spinners that create a splash when they hit the water surface, which helps attract the attention of any nearby bass, and then emit a gurgling noise as they are retrieved, hopefully enticing a fish to bite. Vibrating plugs are also great bass getters. As with buzzbaits, they make noises attractive to bass as you reel them in. Vibrating plugs come in sinking and floating versions, the choice depending on where in the water column the bass are holding. Plastic worms are another standard, and are very effective. Cast these out into the water and let them sink. Keep the line fairly tight so you can feel any strikes. Bright colors tend to work best.

Because largemouth bass like cover and structure, you will be able to fish more of the pond's bass habitat from a float tube or pontoon boat. From just offshore, work the edges of the pond, casting toward the brushy banks. Bass like to hang out around cover, such as that provided by brush and overhanging trees, but will also feed out in more open water within easy reach of cover, where they can escape if they feel threatened. For this reason, don't just concentrate on the edges. Make shorter casts to the more open water 20 or 30 feet out from the shore as well.

Also, as you float around, watch for underwater structure such as stumps, logs, and branches, and thoroughly fish those

Wilsonville Pond is a nice bass, bluegill, and bullhead fishery located right off I-5.

areas as well. A good pair of polarized sunglasses will really help you find these bass habitat hot spots that might otherwise go unnoticed.

If you're a warm-water fly angler, Wilsonville Pond is a good place to pursue largemouth bass with streamers and floating poppers. Use the same approach as you would with plugs and spinners, casting your fly toward the pond's edges and around structure. The same kinds of flies that catch big trout also work quite nicely for largemouth bass. Some favorites include leech patterns, Woolly Worms, Woolly Buggers, and Muddler Minnows. Popper flies can be especially effective for largemouth. Cast them out and then retrieve them to cause them to "pop" as they go through the water—that's when your bass will strike.

Even though bass like to hang around cover, they are out in the open water as well, so don't ignore the other 90 percent of Wilsonville Pond. Open, featureless water is harder to read and it's more difficult to determine where the bass might be, so bass anglers have developed the fan technique whereby you cast your lure methodically in a fan shape from left to right until you have fished all the water in front of you. You then move to a new location and repeat the procedure. The key principle here is the more water you cover, the more fish you are likely to catch. It requires some patience, but if you keep at it, you will catch more fish in the long run.

If you don't have access to a small, portable watercraft, you can still have good fishing from the bank. You can use the fan method to fish the open water in front of clearings on the bank, and you can also fish the shoreline to some extent by casting your lure left and right from your position along the bank and reeling it back in.

The pond's small bluegills can also provide some fun fishing. Fish for them in the same general locations as for largemouth bass, but switch to small spinners and spoons. They can also be caught with bait under a bobber—worms, marshmallows, and PowerBait are favorites. Bluegills can also be great fun to catch with light fly rods, such as 2- and 4-weight outfits, and smaller versions (#10 and #12) of the same flies and poppers you might use for largemouth bass.

Brown bullhead probably offer the most relaxing fishing opportunities at Wilsonville Pond, and because fishing for them generally gets better toward the end of the day as darkness falls, it makes a perfect quarry for those who want to get in a little fishing after leaving work. Brown bullhead are bottom-dwelling fish that like muddy and weedy pond bottoms and can survive in waters with lower oxygen levels than many other fish species, which is why they do so well in small, still waters like Wilsonville Pond.

A variety of baits such as nightcrawlers, chicken liver, and PowerBait are used to catch brown bullhead. Some bullhead anglers claim that chumming the area you are going to focus on will attract more bullhead from other parts of the pond, but having a good, smelly bait on your hook will probably accomplish the same thing, as brown bullhead rely on their sense of smell rather than eyesight to find food. Aromatic commercial catfish bait is effective for this reason. Because they feed on the bottom, your offering will need to be there also, so make sure to have a weight on your line to keep the bait on the bottom of the pond. Bullhead will sometimes nibble for a while before really chomping the bait, so don't become overanxious and set the hook too soon. And because bullhead fishing is a waiting game, a lawn chair is an essential piece of equipment.

9. Woodburn Pond, Woodburn

Distance from downtown Portland: 31 miles

Approximate driving time: 45 minutes

Species available: Largemouth bass, bluegill, crappie, channel catfish

Best times to fish: Spring and summer

Best fishing method: Casting plugs, spinners, jigs, plastics, streamer flies, poppers from the bank or a float tube, or still fishing with nightcrawlers

Recommended map: Oregon road map

Licensing: Oregon Angling License

Directions: From Portland, drive about 28 miles south on I-5 and take exit 271 for Woodburn. Go left (east) onto Highway 214 and drive about 1 mile, turning left onto Boones Ferry Road. Go 1.1 miles, then turn left onto Crosby Road. Continue on Crosby Road for 0.5 mile and turn right onto Edwin Road. Follow Edwin Road for 0.6 mile until you come to the gated dead end and park. There is a sign and trail that leads a short distance to the pond.

THE FISHING

Located adjacent to I-5 in Woodburn, 14-acre Woodburn Pond is another example of an easily accessible, small Willamette Valley pond that offers fun and productive angling opportunities for both children and adults. One of a number of small fishing ponds owned and managed by the Oregon Department of Fish and Wildlife, Woodburn Pond has largemouth bass, bluegill,

Brushy banks and debris in the water make Woodburn Pond good habitat for bass, bluegill, crappie, and catfish.

crappie, and catfish. Although its shoreline is a bit brushy and treed, a trail leading around the pond allows anglers access to various clear spots to cast. Anglers with a float tube or pontoon boat will be able to fish the entire pond much more thoroughly.

Because Woodburn Pond harbors warm-water fish, the angling gets better as the water warms through the spring and summer, into early fall, and then slows down during the cool, rainy winter months. The largemouth bass become more active in the spring, with the best fishing when the water temperature hits 60°F. This is also when the bass start to come in closer to shore to spawn, making them more easily reached by casting from the bank.

STATE-OWNED FISHING WATERS AND FACILITIES

The Oregon Department of Fish and Wildlife owns and manages a number of wildlife areas, hatcheries, ponds, boat launches, and other public fishing access points throughout the state that every angler should know about to maximize fishing opportunities. A number of ODFW's small ponds can be found within the Willamette Valley along the I-5 corridor, making them very accessible to a large number of Oregon residents. Nearly twenty state hatcheries provide public fishing access, and most of them have facilities for disabled anglers such as fishing platforms. In addition, eighteen state wildlife areas offer public fishing access to streams and rivers that cross or flow adjacent to the properties. ODFW also owns and operates more than forty-five boat launches, permitting even more angling access to Oregon rivers.

Plugs, spinners, plastics, and jigs all work great for largemouth bass here. Plugs that ride the water's surface such as prop baits, crawlers, chuggers, and stickbaits will also work nicely when the water hits that 60-degree mark, especially during the morning hours. Later in the day as the sun casts more direct light on the water, the bass will tend to go a little deeper, where they feel more secure from predators. This is the time when crankbaits, minnow plugs, and vibrating plugs that run below the surface will give you an edge. Plastic baits designed to look like worms, frogs, or crayfish are also worth a try.

Largemouth bass are drawn to cover and structure, in search of both food and security, so when fishing for them, look first for this kind of habitat. The margins of Woodburn Pond have lots of cover, and there are clumps of cover and structure farther out on the water as well, often close enough to reach if you are fishing from the bank. Anglers with float tubes or pontoon boats will have an advantage here over the bank-bound, as they can work their way around the entire pond casting toward the brushy shoreline, including places that may be difficult or impossible to cast to from shore. Nevertheless, good fishing can still be had from the bank as well.

Even though you can't cover as much water while fishing from the bank, you can take a page from the float tuber's book by moving to another location if you feel you have fished one spot long enough without success. If there is structure or cover in the open water close enough to cast to, spend a good amount of time exploring it, even if you lose a lure or two to snags. Even from the bank it is possible to fish shoreline areas where it may be too brushy to physically stand by casting parallel to the bank to your left and right. The more water you fish, the more fish you will catch.

Jigging is another effective and popular approach to catching largemouth bass. To fish a jig correctly, cast it out and let it sink to the pond bottom. Next, reel it in with a series of short retrieves, letting the jig pause briefly in mid-retrieve, and repeat until you have brought it back to shore, bouncing it along the bottom as it goes.

Bluegill and crappie gravitate to the same general habitat as largemouth bass, so techniques for catching these fish are very similar, except that smaller spinners and jigs are the preferred lures. Worms and mealworms under a bobber is also a fun way to catch these feisty little game fish.

Fly fishing will also take bass and panfish here, although due to the brushy banks, fishing from a float tube or pontoon boat is preferable since it will give you more room for your backcast. Fish the same locations as you would if you were using any other lure. Good bets include Woolly Buggers, Woolly Worms, Muddler Minnows, and popper flies; larger sizes for bass and smaller for crappie and bluegill.

To catch catfish, all you need are nightcrawlers or PowerBait on a hook and held on the bottom with a weight, along with the patience to wait for them to come along as they search the pond bed for a meal.

10. St. Louis Ponds

Distance from downtown Portland: 37 miles

Approximate driving time: 1 hour

Species available: Rainbow trout, crappie, bluegill, largemouth bass, channel catfish

Best times to fish: Spring through fall

Best fishing method: Casting spinners, plugs, and jigs or bait from the bank

Recommended map: Oregon road map

Licensing: Oregon Angling License

Directions: From Portland, drive south on I-5 for about 30 miles. Take exit 271 and turn right (west) onto Newberg Highway and go about 1 mile. Turn left onto Butteville Road and stay on it for about 3 miles until you enter Gervais and it becomes Ivy Avenue. Turn right onto Fourth Street and go about 4 blocks to Douglas Avenue NE. Turn right and continue on Douglas Avenue NE, which becomes St. Louis Road NE, for 2.3 miles. Turn left onto Tesch Lane just before the railroad tracks, and drive about 1 mile down the gravel road to the St. Louis Ponds parking and picnic area.

THE FISHING

St. Louis Ponds is a great fishing location located in a wooded parcel of the Willamette Valley surrounded by farmlands. It usually offers very good odds of catching fish, particularly stocked rainbow trout, although crappie, bluegill, largemouth bass, and channel catfish are well represented here too. It is an especially good place to take the kids fishing.

St. Louis Ponds

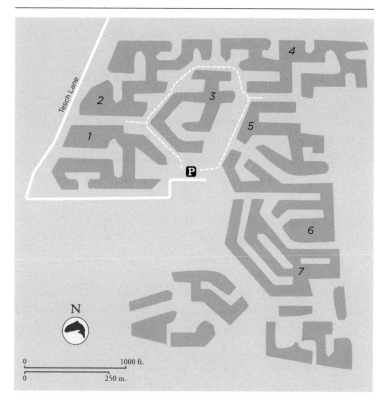

There are seven ponds, including three with fishing platforms suitable for disabled anglers, and an Americans with Disabilities Act (ADA)–compatible trail that provides access to all the ponds. The parking area has restrooms, picnic tables, and small shelters. Part of the 240-acre area is owned by Marion

County, but most is owned and managed by the Oregon Department of Fish and Wildlife. During the summer there is an on-site caretaker, but in the off-season (October 1 to March 1), the road is gated, requiring a walk of about 0.25 mile to reach the parking area. Fishing is allowed here year-round, and the ponds are open from dawn to dusk.

Pond numbers 1, 3, and 6 have ADA fishing platforms. An ADA trail leads from the main parking area to pond 6, around pond 3, and provides access to the remaining five ponds as well. Ponds 1, 3, and 6 contain rainbow trout, crappie, bluegill, largemouth bass, and channel catfish. All the other ponds have warm-water species only. The seven ponds total about 54 acres of fishable water and 7 miles of shoreline from which to fish from the bank. Boats, float tubes, and other floatation devices are not allowed on any of the ponds.

The pond immediately adjacent to the parking area tends to get the most fishing pressure, mainly because it is the closest to facilities and is encircled by grass, with room for lots of anglers and plenty of space to cast. However, good angling can be found in all the ponds. Which one, or ones, you want to fish will probably be based on whether or not you are specifically after trout. Spring is probably the best time for trout fishing at St. Louis Ponds.

The hatchery-origin trout here are usually not too difficult to catch, and the standard approaches of lures and bait will be effective. For lures, use smaller-size spinners—1½ to 3 inches long. Any of the popular brands will work, such as Panther Martin, Mepps, Luhr-Jensen, and Blue Fox. An assortment of lures in different colors is good to have on hand so you can use

FAMILY FISHING EVENTS

St. Louis Ponds is one of the more than three dozen locations in the state that host a family fishing event each year, usually in early spring. Sponsored by the Oregon Department of Fish and Wildlife, these events are designed to introduce youths to fishing and encourage families to fish together. Fishing equipment is provided for participants along with instruction on how to bait hooks, cast a line, and reel in the catch. Adults who want to improve their fishing skills can also get tips from expert anglers on gear, casting techniques, and fish identification.

In addition to family fishing events, another popular event held by the Oregon Department of Fish and Wildlife is the Free Fishing Weekend, which takes place the first weekend after the first Monday in June at various locations throughout the state. This event is also intended to introduce kids to angling and to give them the basic skills to go out and have fun catching fish on ponds, lakes, and streams.

For more information on these events, contact the Oregon Department of Fish and Wildlife.

brighter colors when the sky is overcast or rainy, and have a range of different ones to try on days when the trout are being finicky.

These small ponds are mostly open water, so the approach with lures is a pretty straightforward affair of casting and retrieving, and then moving to another location if the spot you

Rainbow trout are the primary draw for anglers at St. Louis Ponds, but there are opportunities to catch a variety of warm-water species here.

are fishing doesn't produce any bites after a while. Remember, a slower retrieve is generally more effective than a fast retrieve, and you can work your lure through different water depths by varying your retrieve speed and by letting the lure sink for a few moments after your cast before starting to reel it back in. This is a good technique to learn and practice, as it greatly increases the amount of water you will be able to fish, including both the surface area and various depths along the water column, and ups the odds that you will put your lure in front of a trout.

Bait fishing for trout is also popular and effective here, and is an especially good technique if you are introducing kids to fishing. A simple bobber setup using worms, salmon eggs, or PowerBait, or bait fished off the bottom are good ways to go. You can plunk by threading a small marshmallow through the hook and up the shank above your worm or other bait, which will cause the worm to float in the water column above your weight, making it more noticeable and attractive to passing trout.

Spinners are also effective here for largemouth bass, as are surface plugs including stickbaits, prop baits, crawlers, and chuggers, especially in the morning and evening. Surface lures generally work best when water temperatures are around 60°F or warmer. For midday bass fishing, go with jigs; plastic baits molded to look like worms, frogs, crayfish, or other bass food; and deeper-water lures such as sinking minnow plugs, crankbaits, and vibrating plugs. To fish jigs effectively from the bank, first cast the jig out and let it sink to the bottom, then reel it in using a series of short retrieves, pausing briefly then repeating. The idea is let the jig bounce along the bottom of the pond as you reel it in.

Concentrate your bass fishing near weeds and submerged logs and brush along the shoreline. Moving from pond to pond specifically looking for this kind of bass habitat will probably bring you more success over the course of the day than fishing in one pond only.

Spring through fall is the best period for bass and panfish fishing at St. Louis Ponds. Crappie and bluegill utilize the same habitat as the bass. The best way to catch these panfish is with a small jig. Put a piece of worm or salmon egg on the hook and fish it under a bobber.

Channel catfish are bottom-dwellers. Catch them by fishing bait off the bottom. Good baits include nightcrawlers and PowerBait. Channel catfish approaching 30 pounds have been caught at St. Louis Ponds.

Southeast of Portland

Southeast of Portland

WASHINGTON

OREGON

MOUNT HOOD
NATIONAL
FOREST

Columbia River

Sandy River

Clackamas River

Willamette River

84

14

84

26

26

205

30

5

30

26

8

205

213

99W

99E

5

212

212

211

224

Vancouver

Portland

Hillsboro

Beaverton

Tigard

Lake
Oswego

Oregon City

Newberg

Sandy

Estacada

11

12

13

14

15

16

17

18

19

20

N

0   10 km.

0   10 mi.

11. Benson Lake, Benson State Recreation Area

Distance from downtown Portland: 30 miles

Approximate driving time: 35 minutes

Species available: Rainbow trout, brown bullhead, white crappie, sunfish, largemouth bass

Best times to fish: Spring and summer

Best fishing method: Casting bait, spinners, jigs, dry flies, wet flies from the bank or a rowboat, small raft, pontoon boat, or float tube

Recommended map: Oregon road map

Licensing: Oregon Angling License

Directions: From Portland, travel on I-84 east for about 30 miles, and take exit 30 just before Multnomah Falls. The exit ramp will take you directly into Benson State Recreation Area.

THE FISHING

This small, developed park is located in the scenic Columbia River Gorge, with I-84 on its northern boundary and steep, forested terrain to the south. The park has restrooms and picnic facilities, but no boat ramp. There is a day-use fee, except in the winter, when the restrooms are closed. This is also one of the locations for the Oregon Department of Fish and Wildlife's Free Fishing Weekend, held each year in early June.

Benson Lake offers fishing for rainbow trout along with a variety of warm-water species including brown bullhead, white crappie, sunfish, and largemouth bass. Easily accessible off the

Easy accessibility off I-84 makes Benson Lake a good angling destination.

interstate highway, the lake has lots of bank access with plenty of casting room, and its small size (23 acres) makes it easily manageable to fish from a small boat, raft, pontoon boat, or float tube. Boats with motors aren't allowed on the lake, but that is just as well because the noise and activity of engine-powered craft on this small body of water would likely make the fishing less successful and enjoyable.

The lake is stocked each spring and early summer with legal- and trophy-size hatchery rainbow trout, making this a great location for both kids and adults. Bait, lures, and flies are all good approaches for catching the trout here. Because there is no obvious structure breaking the surface of the water, your best approach is to fish the lake as thoroughly as possible, a reasonable task considering the lake's size. If one location isn't producing, either pick up and walk a bit farther along the bank or paddle to another section of water. A pair of polarized sunglasses will help you find areas with submerged sticks and other structures that trout like to hang around.

The simplest approach for catching trout is to go with either bait under a bobber or floating bait off the bottom. Good baits include worms, PowerBait, and marshmallows. If you are fishing the latter two baits under a bobber, you will want to add a little weight to them so they will sink. Fishing under a bobber usually works best in the early morning or low-light days when the trout feel more secure coming closer to the surface. Fishing bait off the bottom, or plunking, involves adding a weight 18 inches or so above the baited hook, then casting into the water. The weight will hold your line in one place while the bait sways in the water, hopefully eventually attracting the attention of nearby fish. Make sure you have plenty of extra hooks, weights, and bait if you are plunking, as the odds are you will snag your line on the bottom and lose some gear over the course of the day's fishing.

For lures, use smaller spinners about 1½ to 3 inches long. Panther Martin, Mepps, Luhr-Jensen, and Blue Fox spinners, spoons, and similar lures all work. The trout usually aren't all that fussy. Because you are fishing mainly featureless water, pick a spot and cast and retrieve your lure. If you don't get any strikes after twenty minutes or so, move on. Keep in mind that a slow retrieve is usually more effective than a faster one, but it can also help to vary your reeling speed, which will control

COLUMBIA RIVER SLOUGHS AND BACKWATERS

Benson Lake is one of a series of small lakes, ponds, sloughs, wetlands, and backwaters that can be found along the edges of the Columbia River. Although there was much more of this type of habitat before construction of the hydroelectric dams on the river, these wetlands still play an important role in the river's ecology and its wildlife, especially its fish. Marshy, weedy backwaters offer many benefits for Columbia River fish species, including steelhead, salmon, and sturgeon. Aquatic vegetation promotes insect populations on which a variety of fish feed. These areas also provide slack-water resting areas for migrating fish and places for smaller, juvenile fish to mature or seek cover from predators. In addition, sturgeon are known to spawn in some of these sloughs. An intrepid angler willing to do some bushwhacking will often find prime warm-water angling seldom visited by his or her competition.

the depth at which the lure travels. After casting, letting your lure sink for a moment or two before reeling it in can also help attract nearby fish. Also, don't forget the general rule of thumb—brighter, more colorful lures on overcast days, and duller lures on bright days.

This is also a good lake for some still-water fly fishing for trout. Although you can cast from shore, this technique is best done from a boat or other floating device. If trout are rising to a hatch, you can cast to them with dry flies. For the most part, unless you are a dedicated match-the-hatcher, just about any of the standard Western dry-fly patterns will get you results: Parachute Adams, Elkhair Caddis, Parachute Caddis, and Whitlock's Hooper, to name a few.

If the trout aren't rising, you can cast your dry fly and let it float naturally on the lake surface until you get a strike. But it might be a while, and patience is a critical virtue when dry-fly fishing still water. However, more experienced still-water fly anglers will tell you that most of what a trout eats is underwater, and you'll catch a lot more trout—and bigger ones at that—if you make your presentations beneath the surface. That means streamers tied to resemble baitfish that you cast out, then strip in or even troll slowly behind your pontoon boat or float tube. Some good lake streamers include Matukas, Muddler Minnows, and Zonkers. In addition, it would also be worth adding leech, Woolly Bugger, Woolly Worm, and scud patterns to that list, fished in a similar manner.

For crappie, sunfish, and largemouth bass, the most common approach at Benson Lake is a worm under a bobber or a jig baited with a grub. You can fish your jig several different ways. One method is to cast the jig out into the water and pause while it sinks to the bottom. Next, jerk on the line and reel in to pull the jig off the bottom as you retrieve it a short distance. Then stop and let it sink again before repeating the procedure. The idea is to bring the jig back to shore in a series of "hopping" motions. Once you've reeled in, repeat the process. This method works from shore or from a raft or float tube. If you are floating out on the lake, you can also use the highly effective vertical jigging method, by letting your jig sink to or near the bottom, then retrieving it in a series of short jerks combined with reeling. Lastly, you can also troll with a jig. Troll slowly through the open water while jerking your rod tip to keep the jig hopping along the bottom. Add a soft plastic curly-tail to the jig to make it wiggle a little more.

If you would like to try for the lake's brown bullhead, fish for them off the bottom, as you would if you were plunking, but shorten up the space between your weight and the hook. As these fish are bottom-feeders, you don't want your bait floating too high off the lakebed. Good baits for bullhead are night-crawlers, chicken liver, and PowerBait. Once you've cast your offering out into the lake, it's a waiting game, so don't forget your lawn chair.

12. Sandy River, Lewis and Clark State Recreation Site

Distance from downtown Portland: 15 miles

Approximate driving time: 20 minutes

Species available: Chinook salmon, coho salmon, steelhead

Best times to fish: March through June and late August through September for chinook; September and October for coho; January through April for winter steelhead; March through September for summer steelhead

Best fishing method: Casting bait, jigs, corkies, spinners from the bank

Recommended map: Oregon road map

Licensing: Oregon Angling License; Combined Angling Tag (for salmon, steelhead, sturgeon, and halibut); Hatchery Harvest Tag (optional, to catch additional hatchery salmon and steelhead)

Directions: From Portland, drive 15 miles east on I-84 and take exit 18 for Lewis and Clark State Park/Oxbow Regional Park. Go a short distance, then turn left onto Crown Point Highway and drive about 0.2 mile to the developed parking area on the left. There are restrooms here and a boat ramp across the highway. Bank access can be found along the highway across from the parking lot. There is also a parking area on the right just after you exit the interstate that has a 1.7-mile trail to the confluence of the Sandy and Columbia Rivers, with lots of Sandy River bank access in between that you can reach via side trails. This is also a popular area for dog walkers.

Lower Sandy River,
Oxbow Park, Sandy Fish Hatchery

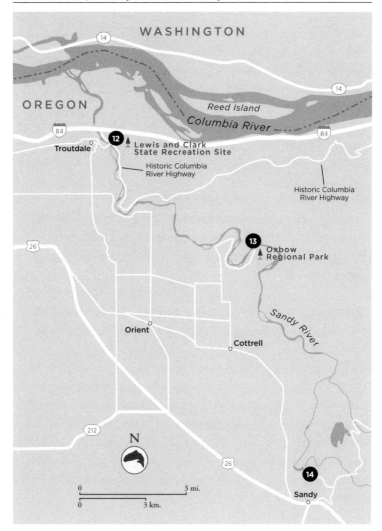

WASHINGTON

14

OREGON

Reed Island

Columbia River

84

Troutdale

12 Lewis and Clark
State Recreation Site

Historic Columbia
River Highway

14

84

Historic Columbia
River Highway

26

13 Oxbow
Regional Park

Sandy River

Orient

Cottrell

212

N

26

14

Sandy

0   3 mi.

0   3 km.

THE FISHING

Although spring chinook are in the lower river as early as March, the fishing doesn't usually start getting really good until a month or two later. The run wraps up in July. There is also a small run of fall chinook late August through October, but these fish are generally not targeted by anglers and are usually caught incidentally. Since they are wild fish, if you catch one, you must release it unharmed.

This bottom reach of the Sandy River through the Lewis and Clark State Recreation Site offers lots of bank access right down to the mouth, which is great because so much successful angling on this river is done from the bank or wading. You can start at either the main parking lot or the lot off the highway and work your way downstream from there. The most popular, and probably the best, approach is floating bait under a bobber. Good baits are nightcrawlers, salmon eggs, and sand shrimp. Use a sliding bobber to adjust the distance from bobber to hook and bait. Adjusting to float the bait around 18 inches off the bottom is the rule of thumb, but some anglers like to cut it closer, skimming the bottom but not quite dragging. A little experimentation with bobber-to-bait ratios will eventually get you to the best formula for the prevailing circumstances.

Equally popular is floating jigs under a bobber. As with floating bait, use a bobber that allows you to easily adjust jig-to-bobber distance. With jigs, setting them to float 18 to 24 inches above the riverbed is usually just about right. Blue, blue and white, and black and purple are good Sandy River jig colors.

The Sandy River at Lewis and Clark State Recreation Site has fishing for Chinook, coho, and steelhead.

Drifting corkies, with bait or a little yarn tied to the hook, is also a standard approach. Use a little weight on your line to keep the bait bouncing off the bottom as it floats downstream. Adjust the weight so the rig floats at about the same speed as the current.

For all three methods, the technique is similar. Toss your line out slightly upstream and let it drift past you downstream until it swings around, then reel in and repeat the procedure. Cover all the water in front of you thoroughly, and if you don't get any action after twenty minutes or so, move on downstream. If you are floating bait or a jig under a bobber, keep a sharp eye out and set the hook if it goes under or does anything unusual.

LEWIS AND CLARK'S FISH

Although Lewis and Clark never ventured up the Sandy River, the intrepid explorers passed by its mouth (where the state recreation site named in their honor is located) in 1805 as they made their way down the Columbia to the Pacific. During the course of their journey down this great river, the explorers got a good introduction to its major fish species, mainly through their dealings with local indigenous peoples. These fish were recorded in their journals as "red charr," salmon trout, white salmon trout, sturgeon, anchovy, "flownder," and "skeet."

Modern historians have studied the descriptions of these fish in the explorers' journals to try to determine exactly what species were being described. Sturgeon was easy enough to confirm, but the others are more challenging. Some researchers think that "red charr" refers to sockeye salmon, while others think it might have been chum salmon. Salmon trout are thought to be steelhead, but the explorers could also have been referring to coho salmon, while white salmon trout are probably coho but perhaps steelhead. The anchovy were undoubtedly the abundant eulachon. The "flownder" and "skeet" were flounder and skate the company observed at the coast.

Despite the abundant fishery resources of the Columbia River, members of the Lewis and Clark expedition preferred elk to fish and only dined on salmon when their hunters failed to return to camp with red meat.

If you are bouncing a corky and bait off the bottom, you'll need to have a feel for the difference between a bite and a bump against a rock or other submerged object.

Mepps Aglias, Blue Fox Vibrax, Uncle Bud's Steelhead Spinners, Rooster Tails, and similar spinners, as well as spoons, will also catch chinook, though more anglers go the bait or jig route. Cast your spinner slightly upstream and then do a slow retrieve, as the lure swings downstream. As it reaches the bottom of the swing, bring it in and repeat the procedure until you feel you have fished all the water in front of you. Make sure you fish the entire run or pool before moving on.

Whether you are fishing bait, jigs, corkies, or spinners, when looking for holding water to cast to, remember that chinook salmon travel deeper in the water column than coho and steelhead, and are more likely to be found in the deeper pools.

Coho fishing on the Sandy is mainly in September and October. All the techniques that work for chinook salmon will catch coho as well. Coho anglers especially like to go with spinners. Blue Fox Vibrax and Luhr-Jensen Sneaks and Bolos are some good coho lures. Good jig colors are lime green, pink, blue, red, orange, brown, and chartreuse. Free-drifting salmon eggs is also worth a try.

Summer steelhead come through from March into September, while the winter run goes from January through April. Use the same methods as for chinook salmon. For spinners, go with Mepps Aglias, Blue Fox Vibrax, Uncle Bud's Steelhead Spinners, and Rooster Tails. Fish pools, around rocks, slots, or any place where steelhead may be resting or traveling. Steelhead can also be found hugging the bank while migrating upstream, so be open to any possibility when choosing what sections of water to fish.

Whether you are after salmon or steelhead, it is worth putting in a little extra time fishing around the mouth of the Sandy River because fish migrating up the Columbia into other systems often stop here to rest for a while, attracted by the cooler freshwater flowing out of the Sandy. The presence of both Sandy River and Columbia River fish ups your odds of success.

13. Sandy River, Oxbow Regional Park

See map on page 74

Distance from downtown Portland: 25 miles

Approximate driving time: 30 minutes

Species available: Chinook salmon, coho salmon, steelhead, rainbow trout

Best times to fish: March through June and late August through September for chinook; September and October for coho; January through April for winter steelhead; March through September for summer steelhead; June through October for rainbow trout

Best fishing method: Casting bait, spinners, jigs, or flies from the bank or wading

Recommended maps: Oregon road map, *Oxbow Regional Park* brochure and map

Licensing: Oregon Angling License; Combined Angling Tag (for salmon, steelhead, sturgeon, and halibut); Hatchery Harvest Tag (optional, to catch additional hatchery salmon and steelhead)

Directions: From Portland, travel east on I-84 for about 15 miles and take exit 17 for Troutdale. At the first stoplight, turn right onto 275th Drive. Go 3 miles and turn left onto Division Street. Continue on Division Street for about 5 miles, following the signs for Oxbow Regional Park. Turn left onto Oxbow Parkway and go 1.6 miles to the park entrance and the fee station. The park road travels along the Sandy River for about 2.5 miles to where it ends at the campground.

The Sandy River is one of Oregon's top steelhead streams, and Oxbow Regional Park offers some of the best public access.

THE FISHING

Managed by Portland Metro, Oxbow Regional Park offers several miles of bank and wading access to the Sandy River, along with picnic areas, a campground, hiking trails, and a boat ramp. River access is via the picnic sites and parking areas you encounter as you initially enter the park, and from trails leading from the east side of the campground on the park's northern terminus, where the river takes a sharp right-hand bend. (You can pick up a brochure with a map from the information kiosk at the park entrance.) While fishing opportunities on the Sandy River include chinook and coho salmon and rainbow trout, it is especially known among anglers for its steelhead fishing, and its winter run in particular.

Spring chinook salmon begin moving into the Sandy River in March. Fishing really starts picking up in May, peaks in June, and then peters out in July. Wild fall chinook are in the river from late August through October but don't provide much of a fishery. Coho salmon are available in September and October. Summer steelhead come through between March and September, with the peak generally in July. Angling for winter-run steelhead goes from January through April, with the largest numbers of fish showing up beginning in February. While rainbow trout are in the river year-round, the trout-fishing season runs from late May through the end of October. Only hatchery fish may be kept. There are also some native, wild cutthroat trout in the river. All wild trout, salmon, and steelhead caught in the Sandy River must be released unharmed.

One important aspect of the Sandy River that anglers should be aware of is that it is a glacier-fed stream, with headwaters on Mount Hood. This means that during warming or rainy periods, runoff from the mountain can cause the river to become very muddy, to the detriment of fishing success. However, it will generally clear off three or four days after an extreme weather event.

A large percentage of spring chinook fishing on the Sandy is done from the bank or wading, and Oxbow Regional Park is among the best locations. While a small number of anglers fish for chinook with flies, most find the best success by floating sand shrimp or eggs under a bobber, or drifting jigs. Although some anglers insist that various shades of pink are the best colors

FREEING THE SANDY RIVER

On October 19, 2007, after years of planning, the Marmot Dam on the Sandy River near the city of Sandy was breached, and the river flowed unimpeded for the first time since 1913. The process to remove the hydroelectric dam began in 1991 when its owner, Portland General Electric, applied to obtain a license renewal from the federal government to operate it. However, due to the high cost of upgrading the dam to allow wild salmon and steelhead to more easily pass upstream to spawn, the company set on a course to remove the structure instead.

Once the river began flowing freely, it started to remake the stream channel. New fish habitat was created when boulders that had been underwater began to poke above the surface, gravel bars were formed, and holes were gouged out of the riverbed. Over time, the river channel and the fish habitat within it will continue to change and improve as the water finds its natural path, unhampered by the old dam. As this natural process unleashed by Marmot Dam's removal continues, it will make the Sandy River a better place for both fish and anglers.

for lures on this river, it will pay to experiment with other hues as well. Fish for fall chinook and coho using the same angling techniques as for spring chinook salmon. Spinners are also a tried-and-true approach for coho.

If you want to try fly fishing for chinook, walk the bank, wading as necessary, and cast to pools using fast-sinking line.

Marabou flies in pink, orange, black, red, and purple are favored for chinook. The Pixie Revenge is a classic salmon fly in this category. Other good chinook salmon flies include shrimp and baitfish patterns such as Humpy flies, the Puget Sound Sand Lance, and Cactus Bugger. Because chinook will hunker down into deep pools beneath faster water during midday, early morning and late afternoon are often more productive times to fish.

The Sandy is one of Oregon's top steelhead rivers, and steelhead fishing probably attracts the largest number of anglers. Drifting bait or a jig under a bobber is a good technique for steelhead here, as is casting spinners, including Mepps Aglias, Blue Fox Vibrax, Uncle Bud's Steelhead Spinners, and Rooster Tails. Look for runs and fish them from head to tailout. Cast your spinner slightly upstream and slowly reel it in, letting your lure swing downstream in the process. Remember, when you get a strike, it will often come at the end of the swing.

Fly fishing for both summer and winter steelhead is extremely popular on the Sandy River. For summer-run fish, floating lines and sinking tip lines and weighted flies work well. Sandy Blue Tubes, Muddler Minnows, Green Butt Skunks, and purple Woolly Buggers are a few favorites for summer steelhead. For winter steelhead, bigger, more colorful flies fished in the classic method—casting slightly downstream across a run and letting the fly swing down and across with the current—produces the best results. Some recommended winter-run flies include the Sandy Candy, Silvey's Squid, Sandy Blue Tube, String Leech, Medusa, Big Red, and pink and orange Agitators.

As a rule of thumb, steelhead typically follow the path of least resistance as they travel upstream. For this reason, among the best places to probe for steelhead with your fly are seams and slots between fast-moving and slower-moving water. Resting areas are also prime places to fish for steelhead. These can include pools and other slow-moving water in between a series of rapids or faster-moving sections of the river. Other good locations are runs, which are pools with a head, body, and tailout. Steelhead like to rest in these runs, with the tailout often being the most attractive location to them. However, during low-water periods the fish may be found in the deeper head of the run, where they feel more secure from predators. Other good places to cast include around boulders and logs and closer to shore where the banks are steep and the water provides a travel channel.

Fishing for stocked rainbow trout—identified by a clipped adipose fin—is also a fun activity on the Sandy. You can use bait such as worms fished off the bottom on this stretch of the river, but many anglers opt for lures or flies. Just about any standard spoon or spinner will work. For fly fishing, any number of standard trout dry flies are productive, including Adams, Elkhair Caddis, and Pale Morning Duns, along with a variety of nymph patterns.

14. Sandy River, Sandy Fish Hatchery

See map on page 74

Distance from downtown Portland: 28 miles

Approximate driving time: 45 minutes

Species available: Chinook salmon, coho salmon, steelhead, rainbow trout

Best times to fish: June through mid-September for chinook; mid-September through early December for coho; November through April for winter steelhead; June through September or October for summer steelhead; June through October for rainbow trout

Best fishing method: Casting bait, jigs, spinners, wet flies from the bank or wading

Recommended map: Oregon road map

Licensing: Oregon Angling License; Combined Angling Tag (for salmon, steelhead, sturgeon, and halibut); Hatchery Harvest Tag (optional, to catch additional hatchery salmon and steelhead)

Directions: From Portland, go 13 miles east on I-84 and take exit 16 for Wood Village. Turn right onto NE 238th Drive. After about 1 mile, NE 238th Drive becomes NE 242nd Drive. Continue on NE 242nd Drive. Proceed about 2 miles, turn left onto East Powell Boulevard, then bear right onto US 26. Follow US 26 for 10 miles to Sandy. Go through Sandy (about 1 mile) and take a left at the stoplight on the east end of town onto Ten Eyck Road. Go 1.2 miles then turn left onto SE Fish Hatchery Road at the sign for the fish hatchery. Go about 1 mile to the fish hatchery and park in the lot at the far end of the facility.

To reach the Sandy River, take the trail at the end of the parking area. The trail begins at an old dirt road and then takes a sharp right turn through a yellow gate, where it becomes a narrow path through the forest. It's a fairly easy, moderate downhill grade about 0.5 mile long to the river. There are a few short steep sections, especially as you drop down into the river's floodplain. You can fish or gain access to the river for wading from a small trail that runs along the bank, though it can be a bit brushy in places. Once you come out on the river, it is about 100 yards downstream to the mouth of Cedar Creek. You can walk the bank and wade both upstream and downstream from this point. However, because the Sandy River's hatchery chinook, coho, and winter steelhead that originate at Cedar Creek Hatchery (on the coast) return via Cedar Creek during the spawning run, angling for these fish takes place from the mouth of Cedar Creek downstream. About a mile of water is accessible to the public before you run into private land. No fishing is allowed in Cedar Creek.

The Fishing

Spring chinook fishing gets going on the Sandy in March, when the fish begin to show up, but the best fishing in the Cedar Creek confluence area takes place June through mid-September. Wild fall chinook are in the river late August through November but don't provide much of a fishery.

Fishing from the bank or wading is the standard approach to spring chinook fishing on the Sandy, and the stretch of

OREGON'S FISH HATCHERY PROGRAM

The Oregon Department of Fish and Wildlife operates more than thirty fish hatcheries, along with a number of acclimation and trapping facilities. These facilities produce nearly ninety different stocks of steelhead, salmon, and trout that are released into Oregon lakes and streams for anglers to catch. In 2009 nearly 44 million fish were released; their combined weight was more than 3.5 million pounds. It costs nearly $30 million per year to operate Oregon's hatchery system. Seventy percent of the funds come from the federal government, 10 percent from the state, and the remaining 20 percent from various other sources. Each hatchery is capable of raising huge numbers of salmon and steelhead. The Sandy Fish Hatchery, for example, annually produces 500,000 coho salmon, 300,000 spring chinook salmon, 180,000 winter steelhead, and 80,000 summer steelhead.

river below Cedar Creek offers lots of good water to explore. Floating salmon eggs or shrimp under a bobber is the most common technique used here and will usually pay off when other strategies fail. Drifting jigs is also worth the effort—try a variety of colors and sizes. A critical factor in drifting jig and bait is to make sure you drift it just off the bottom, with about 18 inches or so off the riverbed the most commonly recommended. Casting spinners such as Mepps Aglias, Blue Fox Vibrax, Uncle Bud's Steelhead Spinners, and Rooster Tails is also a good approach. Look for pools and runs to fish, and cover the water thoroughly before moving on, remembering that chinook salmon like to travel deeper in the water column than steelhead and coho.

The hatchery coho run this reach of the river from mid-September to as late as early December. In some years the numbers of fish can be huge, offering great fishing opportunities as the coho stack up around and just below the mouth of Cedar Creek, following their homing instincts up the creek to the hatchery. Because the Sandy can run a little milky due to glacial melt in its high-country headwater streams around Mount Hood, the coho can be a bit easier to catch here than in streams that are clearer and the fish more easily spooked.

An angler fishes for winter steelhead at the mouth of Cedar Creek.

The coho salmon run can be greatly influenced by rain and river water levels. A big pulse of rain that sends cold freshwater downstream can cause the fish to move upriver rapidly, and in large numbers, so watch the weather reports during the coho run to make sure you don't miss the best action.

You can use the same techniques for coho as for chinook, with floating bait under a bobber and drifting jigs under a bobber the two most common. However, spinner fishing is also a popular technique. Though less commonly employed, you can also catch coho using the traditional jigging method involving casting, letting your jig sink to the bottom, then jerking the line, and repeating until you have reeled all the way in. This technique works best in slower, deeper water—especially pools. Brown, orange, chartreuse, lime green, red, pink, and blue are all good coho jig colors. Unlike chinook, coho tend to travel closer to the surface, so keep that in mind.

Steelheading remains one of the big draws on the Sandy, especially for winter steelhead. Since all Sandy River hatchery winter steelhead are released from the Sandy Hatchery and return to it during their spawning run, you will want to fish for them from the mouth of Cedar Creek downstream. Winter steelhead are in this section of the Sandy late November through April, with the greatest number beginning to arrive in February. The best summer-run steelhead fishing takes place here June through September or October.

You can use a whole range of techniques similar to salmon fishing to catch both summer and winter steelhead. Casting spinners, floating bait under a bobber, and drifting jigs are all good ways to go. Fish the seams between fast and slow water;

around structures such as logs, boulders, and stumps (coho like to hang out in these places too); and pools, making sure to cover their entire length from head to tailout.

This is also a good stretch for fly fishing for steelhead, which is becoming increasing popular on the Sandy River. Fish the seams, slots, pools, and around in-water structures. Some favorite steelhead flies are the Medusa, Big Red, Sandy Candy, String Leech, Silvey's Squid, Sandy Blue Tube, and pink and orange Agitators. But old steelhead standbys such as the Surgeon General, Green Butt Skunk, and Purple Peril will work too.

There are also rainbow and cutthroat trout in the Sandy River. You can catch them with spinners and flies; however, the main attraction of this reach of river is its salmon and steelhead angling opportunities.

15. Clackamas River, Barton Park

Distance from downtown Portland: 23 miles

Approximate driving time: 40 minutes

Species available: Chinook salmon, coho salmon, steelhead, rainbow trout

Best times to fish: April through July for spring chinook; August through October for coho; December through July for steelhead

Best fishing method: Casting bait, spinners, jigs, and flies from the bank or wading

Recommended map: Oregon road map

Licensing: Oregon Angling License; Combined Angling Tag (for salmon, steelhead, sturgeon, and halibut); Hatchery Harvest Tag (optional, to catch additional hatchery salmon and steelhead)

Directions: From Portland, drive south on Highway 99E for about 5.5 miles to Milwaukie, then go 5 miles south on Highway 224 to Clackamas. From Clackamas, continue on Highway 224 for 12.3 miles, then turn right onto Bakers Ferry Road at the sign for Barton Park. At 0.1 mile, where Bakers Ferry Road curves right, continue straight into the park. There is a fee booth at the entrance adjacent to the park office. Follow the park road down a curvy hill to the river floodplain and past two parking areas on either side of the road. Numerous picnic areas and parking on the left allow bank access to the river. Continue on to the end of the road, where there is a parking lot, boat ramp, and bank with riprap, which also provides good fishing access, about 1 mile from the park entrance.

Barton Park offers excellent access to the Clackamas River for a variety of angling techniques.

THE FISHING

Barton Park, run by Clackamas County, offers outstanding angling access to the Clackamas River, including bank access for spinner and fly anglers adjacent to the picnic areas, a high bank with riprap at the terminus of the park road well suited for plunking, and a boat ramp that is a popular put-in for the 5-mile float down to Carver Park.

Fishing on the Clackamas River centers on salmon, steelhead, and rainbow trout. The spring chinook salmon run goes from mid-April into July, while coho salmon come through beginning in August and can provide angling opportunities as late as October, depending on rainfall and water levels. The summer steelhead run begins in April and lasts through July. The winter steelhead run starts in December and goes through April, usually peaking around the middle of January. There are also rainbow trout in the river. Only salmon, steelhead, and trout originating from a hatchery, and indicated by a clipped adipose fin, may be kept. All wild fish must be released unharmed.

The riprap bank by the boat ramp is a good location to plunk for spring chinook and steelhead. Spin-n-Glos are favored by plunkers. While everyone has a favorite method, a typical plunking rig uses a three-way swivel on the end of the line, with a foot-long leader attached to the right-angled swivel. Tied to that is a 3- or 4-ounce weight (although weight sizes will vary depending on how fast the current is flowing at the time). Then, attached to the remaining swivel is a 3- to 4-foot leader with a Spin-n-Glo and hook at the terminus. Orange and chartreuse are popular colors, and some anglers like to also add salmon eggs or colored yarn for additional enticement.

This is also a good spot for fishing with bait or a jig under a bobber, if there aren't too many other anglers along the bank to get tangled up with. Sand shrimp and salmon eggs are the most popular baits. For jigs, experiment with a variety of colors and color combinations over the course of the day to see what works best. Make sure to use a sliding bobber so you can adjust your bait or jig to float 18 to 24 inches off the riverbed. Don't let your bait drag on the bottom.

For coho salmon, drifting eggs with corkies and yarn is one of the more popular approaches on the Clackamas, with favorite colors including red, peach, chartreuse, and blue metallic. Floating bait under a bobber is also effective. Casting spinners is a particularly good way to catch coho on the Clackamas. Bolos and Sneaks, made by Luhr-Jensen, and Blue Fox Vibrax are among the top-rated lures. Go with brighter colors on overcast days or in murkier water, and darker, duller colors when it is bright out or the water is clear or shallow. Because a spurt of rain and the freshet it results in can spur coho to head upstream very quickly, it's important to keep an eye on the weather forecast to make sure you are on the water when the fish are moving and don't miss the bulk of the run altogether.

The same techniques used for chinook and coho salmon will catch steelhead. Mepps Aglias, Blue Fox Vibrax, Uncle Bud's Steelhead Spinners, and Rooster Tails are all good steelhead spinners. For floating jigs under a bobber, black-and-white and pink color combinations seem to catch the most fish.

There is some fly fishing for both chinook and coho on the Clackamas River, with eggs and streamers being typical patterns for these fish. Darker patterns seem to work better here.

Many Clackamas River steelheaders focus on fly fishing. To fly fish for steelhead, park along one of the picnic or group shelter access points and walk the bank, wading as necessary. When searching out places to present your fly, look for seams indicating the transition zone between fast and slow water, pools, and areas around semi-submerged rocks and logs where steelhead may be traveling or resting. Tailouts at the ends of long pools are some of the best places to find steelhead.

The classic steelhead run is water about 3 feet deep and moving about the speed of an average walking pace. Cast your line at a 45-degree angle downstream and let your fly swing around. Make a few more casts, then move a step or two downriver

CLACKAMAS RIVER FISH HISTORY

As with many rivers in Oregon, the history of salmon and steelhead in the Clackamas River is a story of abundance, decline, and now slow but steady recovery. The river once boasted strong historical runs of spring and fall chinook salmon, coho salmon, and winter steelhead, along with native resident trout populations. But the runs of anadromous fish started to decline in the mid-1800s due to commercial overharvesting in the Columbia and lower Clackamas Rivers. In addition, settlement of the region by early pioneers resulted in the degradation of fish habitat along the Clackamas and its tributaries. Dams were also built on the lower river, which impeded spawning runs.

In the late 1870s the drop in fish numbers was so worrisome that the fish cannery industry began to develop a hatchery program to boost the runs. By the early 1940s things began to turn around for the better as fish ladders were installed at the dams and the number of eggs taken from wild Clackamas River salmon and steelhead for propagation at fish hatcheries was reduced. Fish managers began an intensive stocking program in the 1950s and 1960s that has helped the river become an important fishery once again, although its wild, naturally spawning salmon and steelhead remain at risk.

and cast again. Repeat the procedure until you have covered the entire run. In steelhead fishing, it's imperative to fish the water as thoroughly as possible, from the head of the run to the tailout, if you want to be successful. The usual wet flies, along with nymphs with strike indicators, are used for Clackamas River steelhead, including egg patterns and leech and Intruder patterns in red and pink, and black and blue color combinations. Green Butt Skunks, Purple Perils, Surgeon Generals, and Comets (an especially good winter steelhead pattern) are also great, tried-and-true steelhead getters.

Although the bulk of the fishing effort on the Clackamas centers on anadromous fish, there are also good angling opportunities for rainbow trout. Look for them in the same general locations that you would for their seagoing cousins, steelhead. Small spinners and spoons are popular, as are flies. Elkhair Caddis, Adams and Parachute Adams, Woolly Worms, Woolly Buggers, bead-head nymphs, and grasshopper imitations (especially in late summer and fall) are just a few of the recommended patterns for trout.

16. Clackamas River, Carver Park

Distance from downtown Portland: 18 miles

Approximate driving time: 25 minutes

Species available: Chinook salmon, coho salmon, steelhead, rainbow trout

Best times to fish: April through July for spring chinook; August through October for coho; December through July for steelhead

Best fishing method: Drifting bait or casting jigs and spinners from the bank

Recommended map: Oregon road map

Licensing: Oregon Angling License; Combined Angling Tag (for salmon, steelhead, sturgeon, and halibut); Hatchery Harvest Tag (optional, to catch additional hatchery salmon and steelhead)

Directions: From Portland, drive south on Highway 99E for about 5.5 miles to Milwaukie, then go 5 miles south on Highway 224 to Clackamas. From Clackamas, continue on Highway 224 for 7 miles to Carver. In downtown Carver, turn right onto Springwater Road and cross the bridge over the Clackamas River. At the stop sign, turn left onto South Springwater Road and go 0.1 mile. Turn left into Carver Park.

THE FISHING

Although bank access to the Clackamas River at Carver Park may not be extensive, it is easily accessible and is good fishing water. The park has a boat ramp, which is used by drift boat

IMPROVING FISH HABITAT IMPROVES FISHING

Good fishing requires good habitat. Watershed councils, government agencies, and fishing and conservation organizations put time and money into making Oregon creeks and rivers better places for fish to thrive. Clear Creek, which flows into the Clackamas River at Carver Park, is a good example. Clear Creek has been identified by fisheries biologists as the tributary of the Clackamas River that produces the most wild coho salmon and steelhead, using it as both a spawning area and a place for the young fish to grow until they are ready to migrate to the ocean.

To improve Clear Creek's fish habitat, a group of people, including government biologists, conservationists, loggers, and local landowners, got together and put large logs into the creek at ten locations. These logs provide places for the young fish to hide from predators, shade to cool the water during the summer, and the pools, riffles, and other habitat conditions that salmon and steelhead need to prosper. Although these fish are wild and must be released when caught, they are an important facet of Clackamas River recreation.

anglers for the popular float from Barton Park, along with a good-size parking lot, restrooms, and picnic tables. River bank access is behind the restroom area, but you can also fish from the boat ramp when boaters are not using it.

The Clackamas River has runs of spring chinook salmon, coho salmon, and both summer and winter runs of steelhead.

There is also good angling for hatchery, adipose fin–clipped rainbow trout.

Spring chinook begin entering the river by the middle of April and continue into July. This run tends to peak in late May or early June. Coho salmon, which originate in the Eagle Creek Hatchery, begin coming into the Clackamas in August and can move upstream and back to the hatchery within a couple of weeks or so if there is lots of rain that brings a freshet. More typically, however, they provide fishing well into September and October. Winter steelhead are available December through April, peaking in mid-January, while the summer run is in the river April through July. The hatchery rainbow trout are present year-round.

Although not extensive, Carver Park provides convenient bank access to the Clackamas River.

Only fin-clipped trout, salmon, and steelhead are allowed to be harvested on the Clackamas River; all wild fish must be released. Rainbow trout over 20 inches in length are considered to be steelhead, and if you catch one that doesn't have a clipped adipose fin, you need to let it go.

The most popular technique for catching spring chinook is drifting bait under a bobber, or drifting jigs. Sliding bobbers are the preferred type for salmon (and steelhead) fishing, as you can move them up and down your line to easily adjust the depth that your bait or jig will float. Because chinook salmon tend to travel deeper in the water column, floating your offering 1 or 2 feet off the riverbed is about right. A sliding bobber will make fine-tuning your bait or jig depth easier to do. For bait, try salmon eggs or sand shrimp. Marabou jigs are a favorite, and some anglers like to add a bit of salmon roe or sand shrimp to the hook on their jig for added enticement. The technique is pretty straightforward and can be done with either a bait-casting or spinning outfit. Just cast out upstream and let it float by. Keep a sharp eye on your bobber, and set the hook if it starts to go underwater or behaves erratically. As always, work the water in front of you thoroughly, and if a half hour or so goes by with no action, move to another location along the bank.

The quality of the coho salmon fishing depends a great deal on water levels, as rainy weather and the pulse of freshwater it sends downstream will cause the fish to move upriver, sometimes very rapidly. Be sure to watch the weather forecast as you plan your coho fishing trip. Floating salmon eggs under a bobber seems to be the best approach for catching coho on the Clackamas River, though some anglers like to cast spinners as well.

For summer steelhead, drifting bait and jigs as for chinook is a preferred method. However, spinners are equally favored. You generally will want to use lures that are less bright and flashy so as not to spook the fish in clearer water on sunny days, but they also need to shine enough underwater to attract a steelhead into striking. For this reason, make sure you have a good selection of spinners with you, including different colors and finishes. The standard technique is to cast slightly upstream, then bring your lure in with a slow retrieve, allowing it to swing downstream as you reel in. The strike often comes at the bottom of the swing, so stay alert as your line reaches that point.

Although the majority of winter steelheaders drift fish, Carver Park offers some of the better bank-fishing opportunities for this run. A favorite location is where Clear Creek flows into the Clackamas River at Carver Bridge, which is the bridge you cross to reach the park. Most of the winter steelhead are usually caught here by drifting bait or corkies and yarn, though spinners are worth a try as well. Floating jigs under a bobber is also productive, with pink, black, and white color combinations reputed to be the best. During the winter when the water is higher and likely to be a little murkier, brighter, flashier spinners will probably bring better results.

Carver Park is also a nice spot for some relaxed trout fishing. Casting small spinners is the best approach, and favorites include Mepps Aglias, Blue Fox Vibrax, and Rooster Tails. (These spinners, along with Uncle Bud's Steelhead Spinners, in sizes #3 or #4 are also popular lures for salmon and steelhead.) Most of the trout in the Clackamas are rainbow trout, but you may encounter a few brown and brook trout as well.

17. Willamette River, Meldrum Bar Park

Distance from downtown Portland: 12 miles

Approximate driving time: 25 minutes

Species available: Chinook salmon, coho salmon, steelhead, shad, sturgeon, smallmouth bass

Best times to fish: March into July, peaking mid-April through mid-May, for spring chinook; September and October for fall chinook; September through November for coho; March through September for summer steelhead; December into March for winter steelhead; sturgeon year-round; June through August for shad; spring and summer for smallmouth bass

Best fishing method: Plunking with bait or Spin-n-Glos or casting spinners, shad darts from the bank

Recommended map: Oregon road map

Licensing: Oregon Angling License; Combined Angling Tag (for salmon, steelhead, sturgeon, and halibut); Hatchery Harvest Tag (optional, to catch additional hatchery salmon and steelhead); Two-Rod Angling License (optional, to use two rods at the same time)

Directions: From Portland, drive south on SE Martin Luther King Jr. Boulevard for about 1.5 miles. Martin Luther King Jr. Boulevard merges into SE Grande for about 0.3 mile, then becomes SE McLoughlin Boulevard (Highway 99E). Continue for about 9 miles and turn right onto SE Glen Echo Road. Go about 0.1 mile, then bear left onto SE River Road and continue for 0.5 mile. Turn right onto Meldrum Bar Park Road. Continue past the ball fields and follow the road for about 0.4 mile to the parking area and boat ramp. At the bottom of the hill, jutting downstream, is Meldrum Bar. You can drive your vehicle out onto the bar, though it may not be accessible during high-water periods. The park is located in Gladstone.

THE FISHING

Meldrum Bar is a very popular fishing location, particularly for salmon and steelhead, and somewhat of a unique fishery due to its location on a narrow gravel bar in the river. Because it can be very busy with anglers, especially during peak salmon and steelhead runs, fishing is generally limited to plunking. The reason for this is that using other techniques, such as drifting

A winter steelhead angler fishes with Spin-n-Glo on the Willamette River at Meldrum Bar Park.

FLOODING AND FLOODPLAINS

Much of the Willamette Valley through which the Willamette River flows is floodplain. Floodplains are a vital part of a river, and critical to the survival of salmon, steelhead, and other fish. A floodplain is simply a flat area along a river where water spills over during floods. For any human structures in the way, floods are bad news. But, ecologically, flooding is one of the best things that happen to rivers and the fish that swim in them.

When water overflows the banks of a river, it scours out the floodplain, creating gravel bars, alcoves, side channels, and other features that provide important habitat for salmon and steelhead. Repeated flooding of an area deposits layers of nutrient-rich soil, which fosters a diversity of plants that benefit many species. Perhaps most important, a floodplain acts as a safety valve that allows flooding water to spread out over a broader area where it loses much of its force, reducing the damage the rising water might otherwise do to human habitation and the river corridor.

or floating bait and jigs, will tangle with other anglers' lines downstream and make you an unpopular addition to the group.

You can plunk with bait using the typical setup: a three-way swivel on the end of your line, with a foot-long leader attached to one swivel terminating with enough weight to keep it anchored to the bottom (depending on the speed of the river's current), and a 3- to 4-foot leader on the other swivel to which you attach your hook baited with salmon roe or sand shrimp. A lot of Meldrum Bar anglers also like to plunk with Spin-n-Glos, sometimes adding sand shrimp or a piece of yarn as added enticement. You will also want a rod holder and lawn chair (or you may want to sit in your vehicle if it is raining) as plunking is a waiting game, and you will need to have the patience to let your rig sit out in the water for extended periods before getting a bite. Many Meldrum Bar anglers attach bells to the tips of their rods to alert them when they have a fish.

You can also try casting spinners, especially for steelhead and coho, but be sure you have enough leeway between your neighbors so you don't interfere with their fishing. Winter steelhead anglers often do very well at Meldrum Bar when the water is high and muddy, and the steelhead travel and hold near the bank.

Sturgeon are available here year-round, though the best fishing seems to be in May and June. Fish for them in deep holes, with a stout rod-and-reel rig, heavy weight, and eel, herring, smelt, or sand shrimp for bait. Keep in mind that the state manages sturgeon on a quota system, which can result in midseason rule changes, so be aware of the current situation before going sturgeon fishing.

Shad come through June through August, and the standard method used to catch them is casting shad darts or small spinners with a light- to medium-weight spinning outfit. There is also a nice smallmouth bass fishery on this stretch of the Willamette River. For smallmouth bass, cast Rooster Tails and similar colorful, splashy lures. They like rocky areas, riffles, and sections of the river with a faster current, where the water is more oxygenated, but you might also find them in slack-water areas and holes, where they will sometimes congregate.

18. Willamette and Clackamas Rivers, Clackamette Park

Distance from downtown Portland: 12 miles

Approximate driving time: 25 minutes

Species available: Chinook salmon, coho salmon, steelhead, shad, smallmouth bass, sturgeon

Best times to fish: March into July, peaking mid-April through mid-May, for spring chinook; September and October for fall chinook; September through November for coho; March through September for summer steelhead; December into March for winter steelhead; sturgeon year-round; June through August for shad; spring and summer for smallmouth bass

Best fishing method: Plunking with bait and Spin-n-Glos or drifting bait and corkies, or casting spinners or shad darts from the bank

Recommended map: Oregon road map

Licensing: Oregon Angling License; Combined Angling Tag (for salmon, steelhead, sturgeon, and halibut); Hatchery Harvest Tag (optional, to catch additional hatchery salmon and steelhead); Two-Rod Angling License (optional, to use two rods at the same time)

Directions: From Portland, go south on SE Martin Luther King Jr. Boulevard for about 1.5 miles. Martin Luther King Jr. Boulevard merges into SE Grande for about 0.3 mile, then becomes SE McLoughlin Boulevard (Highway 99E). Continue for about 10 miles, then turn right onto Dunes Drive and go a few hundred feet. Turn right onto Clackamette Drive for 0.1 mile to the entrance to Clackamette Park. Clackamette Park is in Oregon City.

THE FISHING

Anywhere that two rivers converge is likely to be a good place to fish, and that rule certainly applies to Clackamette Park, where the Clackamas River flows into the Willamette.

Chinook salmon are one of the big draws for anglers—spring chinook from March into July, peaking mid-April to mid-May, and fall chinook in September and October. Plunking with bait or Spin-n-Glos is one of the most effective ways to go here.

Located at the mouth of the Clackamas and Willamette Rivers, Clackamette Park offers good fishing in both streams.

THE WILLAMETTE RIVER,
A SALMON AND STEELHEAD HIGHWAY

The Willamette River is one of Oregon's most important waterways and was a major factor in the state's early settlement and economic development. Originating in the mountains southeast of Eugene, the Willamette flows for nearly 190 miles until it empties into the Columbia River at Portland, draining a basin of 11,480 square miles. While the river remains an important travel corridor for human commerce, it is also an important highway for spawning salmon and steelhead moving toward tributary streams in the Cascade and Coast Range mountains. As difficult as that journey has always been for the fish, today it is even more fraught with peril. Pollution, degraded habitat, and stream barriers make the odds of completing their run steep indeed.

Make sure you use enough weight to keep your rig from moving downstream in the current, and set your bait or Spin-n-Glo to float several feet from the river bottom.

For plunking with bait, sand shrimp and salmon eggs are most commonly used. Some anglers like to add a bit of bait or tie a strand of yarn to their Spin-n-Glo setup as an added attractant. The idea of plunking is to put your offering in the salmons' travel path, and sooner or later one will come by and take your hook. Since it might be a while, a comfortable lawn chair to sit in is a good idea. Some anglers like to tie a bell to their rod tip to alert them to strikes. Drifting corkies or bait under a bobber is also a good method here.

Clackamatte Park can offer some very nice coho salmon fishing in late fall and early winter. These fish are headed up the Clackamas River, so you will want to concentrate your efforts around the mouth. While the same methods used for chinook will catch coho, many coho salmon anglers favor casting spinners. Some of the most used coho spinners are Blue Fox Vibrax and Luhr-Jensen Sneaks and Bolos. Any number of other spinners designed for salmon and steelhead will also work, such as Panther Martins and Uncle Bud's. Work the water around the mouth thoroughly, covering as much water as you can. Slower retrieves are usually more effective than faster ones, and keep in mind that coho tend to swim closer to the surface than chinook.

For steelhead, fish the water around the mouth of the Clackamas, where they often hold in the shallow edge areas. Plunking with bait or Spin-n-Glos and casting spinners such as Panther Martins, Mepps Aglias, Blue Fox Vibrax, Uncle Bud's Steelhead Spinners, and Rooster Tails are all good approaches for steelhead at Clackamette Park.

Shad come through on their annual upstream spawning run in July and August. Casting shad darts and spinners is the way to catch them and is largely a matter of getting your lure out in the water, reeling in, and repeating as often and as long as possible, since you are looking to have your lure and a migrating fish eventually meet eye to eye. The longer you keep your lure in the water, the better you will do.

The best fishing for sturgeon is typically in the spring and early summer, but they are here year-round. Fishing bait on the bottom of deep holes is the ticket for catching sturgeon. You'll want a heavy enough weight to keep your bait on the bottom and not drifting with the current. Smelt, herring, sand shrimp, and eel are some of the more typical sturgeon baits. Sturgeon angling is carefully regulated as to seasons and the number of fish that can be harvested each year. Once the harvest quota is reached, the season is ended, so be sure that you are up on the current catch situation and prevailing regulations.

There can also be some good smallmouth bass fishing around the mouth of the Clackamas River. Cast small spinners in faster water, which attracts the fish because of its greater oxygen content, and pools where the bass will sometimes stack up to feed. Smallmouth bass like rocky areas, so look for those too.

19. Eagle Creek,
Bonnie Lure State Recreation Area

Distance from downtown Portland: 21 miles

Approximate driving time: 40 minutes

Species available: Winter steelhead, chinook salmon, coho salmon

Best times to fish: January through March for winter steelhead; July and August for chinook salmon, September and October for coho

Best fishing method: Casting bait, jigs, spinners, wet flies from the bank or wading

Recommended map: Oregon road map

Licensing: Oregon Angling License; Combined Angling Tag (for salmon, steelhead, sturgeon, and halibut); Hatchery Harvest Tag (optional, to catch additional hatchery salmon and steelhead)

Directions: From Portland, drive south on Highway 99E for about 5.5 miles to Milwaukie, then go south 5 miles on Highway 224 to Clackamas. From Clackamas, continue on Highway 224 for about 9.5 miles to the community of Eagle Creek. Turn right onto SE Dowty Road and follow it for a little over a mile, including a curvy downhill section, bearing right to stay on SE Dowty Road until you come to the bridge crossing Eagle Creek. A parking area is located just across the bridge on the right side, where there is a sign for Bonnie Lure State Recreation Area. A narrow trail leads to the creek immediately below the bridge and downstream along the creek. Access to the

Eagle Creek

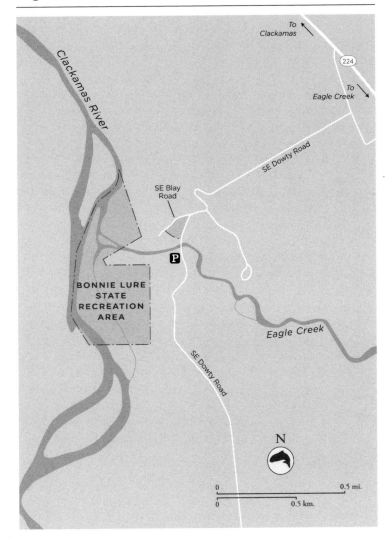

Clackamas River

To Clackamas

224

To Eagle Creek

SE Dowty Road

SE Blay Road

P

BONNIE LURE STATE RECREATION AREA

Eagle Creek

SE Dowty Road

N

| 0 | | 0.5 mi. |
| 0 | | 0.5 km. |

recreation area is also available off SE Blay Road, to the right just before you cross the bridge. There is also about 0.5 mile of public fishing access on the Clackamas River, of which Eagle Creek is a tributary, in the recreation area at the creek's mouth.

THE FISHING

Eagle Creek is a very productive coho salmon and winter steelhead fishery, due primarily to the presence of the Eagle Creek National Fish Hatchery, which raises more than a million coho—350,000 of which are released at the hatchery—and 100,000 winter steelhead annually. When these fish return to the hatchery up Eagle Creek during their spawning runs, the fishing can be very good. This location also offers excellent bank access, on a creek that runs through quite a bit of private property.

This is a bank and wading fishery, and anglers, whether fishing for coho or steelhead, walk the creek edge and work all likely looking water. This includes pools, from head to tail, and around structures such as logs and stumps.

For coho, which generally run up Eagle Creek toward the hatchery in September and October, free-drifting a clump of salmon eggs is a very good technique. Floating jigs under a bobber is also worth putting some time into. Use a sliding bobber so you can adjust your jig to float up off the bottom of the creek. If it drags, you probably won't be catching too many fish. One-eighth-ounce jigs in blues, blue and white, and purple and black are recommended.

Spinners are also a tried-and-true coho catcher. Coho favorites are Blue Fox Vibrax and Luhr-Jensen Sneaks and Bolos. Look for pools and cast slightly upstream, reeling the lure in

Anglers drift bait in Eagle Creek for winter steelhead on a rainy February afternoon.

slowly as it swings downstream. Work the entire pool, including head, body, and tailout. Make sure you carry a good supply of spinners in a variety of colors. You'll want brighter colors when the water is murkier or on overcast or rainy days, and duller-finished ones on bright days or when the water is clear.

You can also go with bait under a bobber, usually a small cluster of salmon eggs or sand shrimp. A little bit of yarn can be added to the hook as well. As with jigs, use a sliding bobber so you can adjust the distance between bait and creek bottom so you don't drag.

Bait fished under a bobber and spinners are how most Eagle Creek chinook salmon are caught.

WILD FISH VS. HATCHERY FISH

The longstanding controversy over fish hatcheries revolves around how much negative impact hatchery-produced salmon and steelhead have on their wild counterparts, and if curtailing hatchery production will result in fewer recreational fishing opportunities.

Because of the huge popularity of steelhead and salmon fishing and the loss of spawning habitat due to human development over the years, hatchery advocates argue that without hatchery fish, there would simply not be enough salmon and steelhead to meet the angling demand. And because wild fish are protected and must be released when caught, anglers would not be able to take a salmon or steelhead home to smoke or barbeque.

On the other hand, wild fish advocates point to the growing body of scientific evidence that shows that when hatchery fish and wild fish spawn together in the wild, they produce less fit offspring, and over time this could contribute to the extinction of wild fish. They say that by helping wild fish populations recover and expand, we will have better fishing in the long run.

Fisheries and hatchery managers have responded with a number of reforms, including using eggs from wild fish to raise in hatcheries, physically keeping hatchery and wild fish from spawning with each other by using barriers and traps, and not stocking hatchery fish in some streams at all. Still, the issue remains controversial and unresolved.

The first winter steelhead start moving into the creek in late November, with fishing starting up in December. However, the bulk of the steelhead fishing generally takes place January through well into March. While the fishing techniques for coho also work on winter steelhead, many anglers lean toward drifting corkies. Corkies are attractors made to look like a clump of salmon eggs and drifted, with a little weight added, through pools. Balance the weight so that the corky floats at about the same speed as the current. Adding bait is also a favored approach, with sand shrimp, salmon roe, and nightcrawlers most preferred. Yarn added to the hook provides some additional enticement.

Cast your setup into holding water, slightly upstream, and let it drift through. Repeat until you feel you have covered that stretch of water thoroughly. When fishing with corkies, you want them to bounce along the bottom a little, but you'll need to develop a feel for telling the difference between a take by a fish and a bump against a submerged rock.

It can't be emphasized enough that the colors you use for various components of your rig can have a major affect on your success rate, dictated by water clarity. The murkier the water, the brighter the colors you should use. Keep a good selection in your tackle box or vest so you will be prepared for any water conditions encountered. If the colors you are using don't seem to be working, switch to something else until you start getting results.

Eagle Creek has some good opportunities for fly fishing for both coho and steelhead, and those methods can be very productive. For coho, try drifting fly patterns that resemble eggs.

For winter steelhead, any of the classic wet and nymph patterns will work, including Woolly Buggers, Muddler Minnows, Green Butt Skunks, and Purple Perils. Fish the runs, tailouts, slots, and around in-stream structures.

While Eagle Creek is generally the focal point of coho and winter steelhead fishing because of the runs returning to the hatchery, you can also fish the Clackamas River downstream of the creek mouth to try to intercept fish before they reach the creek. Use the same angling techniques as you would for Eagle Creek. The run timings are also the same.

20. North Fork Reservoir, Estacada

Distance from downtown Portland: 35 miles

Approximate driving time: 50 minutes

Species available: rainbow, cutthroat, brook, and brown trout

Best times to fish: Summer and fall

Best fishing method: Casting from the bank or trolling from a boat with spinners and spoons, troll rigs with flashers from a boat, or still fishing with bait

Recommended map: Oregon road map

Licensing: Oregon Angling License

Directions: From Portland, drive south on Highway 99E for about 9 miles, then go 20 miles south on Highway 224 to Estacada. Drive through Estacada and continue on Highway 224 for another 5 miles. North Fork Reservoir is on the right. The highway follows the north shoreline, and there are numerous places to access the bank. A parking lot is on the left at the 5.7-mile mark. You can also continue another 0.5 mile to Promontory Park on the right, which has docks, a boat launch, and additional bank access.

THE FISHING

Formed by a dam on the Clackamas River at its confluence with the North Fork Clackamas, North Fork Reservoir is an excellent fishery for stocked rainbow trout, which are planted on a regular basis from mid-spring through early fall. The narrow reservoir is about 4 miles long and 350 acres at full pool, providing plenty of water for anglers to explore from the bank

THE WILD AND SCENIC CLACKAMAS RIVER

Although it may not seem like it while fishing on the tranquil waters of North Fork Reservoir, just a short distance above the reservoir, between Big Cliff and Big Springs, the Clackamas River flows wild through the Mount Hood National Forest. In fact, in 1988 this 47-mile stretch of the river was designated a federal Wild and Scenic River because of its many natural and recreational attributes. The upper river is also important from a fisheries standpoint, as it provides habitat for one of the last runs of wild coho salmon in the Columbia River basin, along with spring chinook salmon and steelhead. The upper river once offered an excellent steelhead fishery, but it has since been closed and is now managed as a wild fish sanctuary. The upper river also has populations of native cutthroat, rainbow, and introduced brook trout.

or by boat. In addition to hatchery rainbow trout, the reservoir has some wild cutthroat, brown, and brook trout, the latter two being nonnative species. Brown trout, brook trout, and adipose fin–clipped rainbow trout (indicating they are hatchery fish) may be kept.

Lots of bank access can be found along the east shoreline, which is paralleled by Highway 224. There is also access to the lakeshore around the North Fork Dam via East Faraday Road on the lower end of the reservoir about 5 miles south of Estacada, on the right. Some of the best and easiest access is at Promontory Park on the reservoir's upper end.

Promontory Park is operated by Portland General Electric, which generates hydroelectric power from North Fork Dam. It is open from the middle of May through mid-September and features a boat ramp, docks, fifty campsites, picnic areas, restrooms and showers, electric cooking facilities, boat rentals, and a small store that sells fishing supplies. There is also a 1-acre pond in the park called Small Fry Lake that is stocked with rainbow trout, with the fishing limited to kids age 14 and younger.

The upper part of the reservoir around Promontory Park tends to have the best fishing, since that is where most of the trout are stocked, and there is abundant access. Because the reservoir's water can still be a bit cool in May and the trout sluggish, June and July tend to provide the best bite. Trout fishing is also good in September and October. Hot August weather can slow the fishing down a little, as the trout head to deeper water to keep cool. In addition, the reservoir can be busy with waterskiers on hot midsummer days, which can complicate fishing a little, especially if you are out on the water in a boat. Another good area is near the boat ramp by the dam on the lower reservoir. This also a good location to take kids fishing.

A whole range of standard trout-fishing techniques will produce here. Since the trout are not especially large—the stocked rainbows are typically in the 8- to12-inch range—you don't need heavy fishing line. Something in the 5-pound-test range will suffice. If you are fishing from the bank, nightcrawlers or PowerBait is often the simplest approach. Corn, marshmallows, and salmon eggs are also good enticements.

You can either fish the bait under a bobber or use a weight and float your offering off the bottom, but there are some things

North Fork Reservoir, near Estacada, is one of the best Portland area trout fisheries.

to keep in mind when deciding which way to go. Fishing with a bobber is generally better during mornings and evenings, or on overcast low-light days when the fish feel more secure coming closer to the surface. One of the advantages of using a bobber is that you can float the bait farther from the bottom and are less likely to get your rig tangled up in weeds or other bottom vegetation and debris. Nightcrawlers work great under a bobber because they sink. However, if you use PowerBait, marshmallows, or other baits that float, you will need to add a little weight, such as some split shot, to keep it hanging below your bobber.

Fishing bait off the bottom, on the other hand, is most effective on bright days when the fish like to hold deeper for safety. A couple of approaches are common here: You can mold PowerBait on a treble hook (or even use a PowerBait and worm combination), or thread a worm on a bait hook—a #8 is a good size. There is no hard-and-fast rule about how far off the bottom to float your bait, but around 18 inches is a good starting point, so put your weight at about that point and cast out. Since your gear will be on the bottom of the lake, your odds of getting hung up on snags and losing hooks are fairly high, so make sure you bring enough extra rigging along to last through the day.

Although most bank anglers prefer bait, you can also cast spinners and spoons. Any of the popular brands such Mepps Aglias, Blue Fox Vibrax, and Rooster Tails will work just fine. Use larger, more colorful lures on overcast days and smaller lures with duller colors and finishes on bright, sunny days. The strategy here is that in lower light, fish will more easily spot the bigger, brighter lures. On bright days when underwater visibility is greater, the fish are more wary of predators, and a smaller, less brightly colored lure is less likely to spook them when it hits the water.

As a rule of thumb, a slower retrieve is more effective than a fast retrieve, but don't be reluctant to vary your speed a little during each retrieve to better mimic the behavior of the baitfish that spinners and spoons are designed to resemble. Don't just keep casting to the same location, but work all the water in front of you. If you aren't getting any action after twenty minutes or so, pick up your tackle box and move on to another spot on the bank.

If you have a boat, you are at an advantage, as you can fish more of the reservoir's water and can use some very effective trolling techniques. There is a boat ramp at Promontory Park and one by North Fork Dam, which is accessed via East Faraday Road on the lower end of the reservoir. While it's worth fishing just about everywhere on the reservoir, a couple of recommended locations for anglers with boats are around the power lines just down-reservoir from where the North Fork Clackamas flows into the reservoir, and by the point just up-reservoir from the lower boat ramp.

Trolling works very well at North Fork Reservoir and will catch a lot of trout. You can keep it simple and just troll small spoons and spinners, but more savvy and successful boat anglers add flashers or other attractors to their rigs, which really ups the odds. Some favorite lake trolls include Beer Cans, Ford Fenders, and School-O-Minnows. To that rig add just about any kind of spinner or spoon, or even a small plug. Some anglers also add a worm as well. Favorites include Kwikfish, Needlefish, Dick Nites, and Super Dupers.

Beyond the rigging, a few basic principles should be followed when trolling for trout. The first is to troll slowly. Lures are designed to work better at slower trolling speeds, and there is a limit to how fast a trout is willing to swim to grab your lure. For trout, a good rule of thumb is to troll at about the same speed you would be going if you were rowing your boat. The second principle is to vary your speed so that your lure runs at different depths depending on how fast you are going. This will also vary the lure's "action," making it more noticeable and enticing to nearby trout. Finally, avoid constantly trolling in a

straight line by doing S curves, which will also vary your lure's depth and action.

On days when the fishing is slow, here are a few tips that might pick things up: Give your line a quick jerk every few minutes as you troll along; double your trolling speed for a short distance, then slow back down quickly. Strikes will most likely happen as the lure is slowing down and dropping deeper into the water column. Finally, if the fish are extra wary, add a longer and lighter leader to your rig to keep from spooking them.

Fishing in Washington State

There are certainly many good fishing opportunities across the Columbia River in Washington State. However, assuming you are an Oregon resident, fishing in another state requires some additional considerations. You will need to purchase a nonresident fishing license and tags, for instance, which are more expensive than for resident anglers. You will also need to familiarize yourself with Washington's fishing regulations, which are not necessarily similar to Oregon's.

That being said, here are a couple of nice Washington waters within an hour's drive of Portland, worth checking out when you are in the mood to venture into some new fishing territory.

Fishing in Washington State

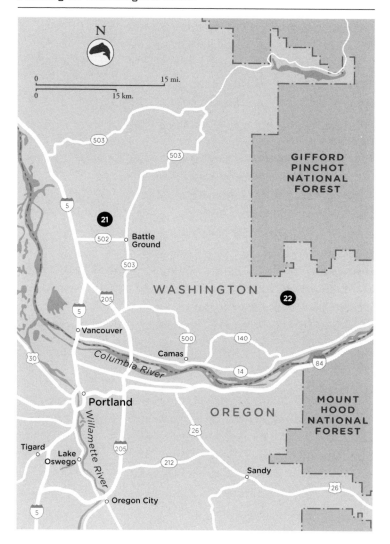

21. East and North Forks Lewis River

Distance from downtown Portland: 35 miles

Approximate driving time: 40 minutes

Species available: Chinook salmon, coho salmon, steelhead

Best times to fish: April through June and September to December for chinook; September to December for coho; mid-April to October and December through mid-February for steelhead

Best fishing method: Casting bait, jigs, spinners, spoons, flies, or flies from the bank or wading

Recommended map: Washington road map

Licensing: Washington Freshwater Fishing License and Catch Card; Columbia River Salmon/Steelhead Endorsement

Directions: Access to the main stem and North Fork is via I-5 and WA 503 at Woodland. Fishing access at Daybreak Park is located on the East Fork in Battle Ground. To reach Daybreak Park, take exit 9 off I-5, about 25 miles north of Portland. Go north on NE 10th Avenue for about 2 miles, turn right onto NE 219th Street and drive 3 miles then turn left onto NE 72nd Avenue. Proceed along NE 72nd Avenue for 2 miles, then bear right onto NE 259th Street. At about 0.5 mile, turn left onto 82nd Avenue and follow it for 0.3 mile to the park on Daybreak Road. Lewisville Park, another access point, is located off WA 503, 2.2 miles north of Battle Ground.

Access for bank anglers and waders is very good on the Lewis River system. There is some bank access along the dike area immediately below the confluence of the North and East

Lewis River

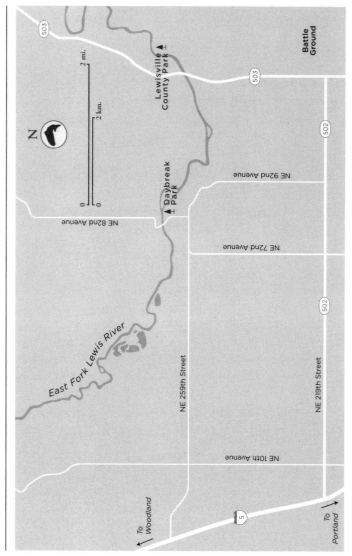

Forks, along with good bank access to the North Fork at the Lewis River Hatchery. Access on the East Fork includes launches at Daybreak Park and Lewisville Park.

THE FISHING

Floating bait under a bobber and plunking with salmon eggs or sand shrimp are popular approaches for spring chinook salmon. The same techniques work for coho as well, with the addition of spinners and spoons.

For steelhead, floating bait such as eggs and sand shrimp is a common technique, but jigs are becoming more prevalent on the Lewis system. The island at Woodland is a favorite location to target steelhead.

Fly fishing is also popular with East Fork Lewis anglers, and the fish will respond to just about any tried-and-true steelhead fly, such as the Kalama Special, Comet, Purple Peril, Skykomish Sunrise, and After Dinner Mint. Holding areas in fast water tend to produce better than deep pools on the East Fork.

22. Washougal River

Distance from downtown Portland: 30 miles
Approximate driving time: 40 minutes
Species available: Chinook salmon, coho salmon, steelhead
Best times to fish: August through October for chinook; late October through November for coho; April to December for steelhead
Best fishing method: Casting bait or spinners and jigs from the bank
Recommended map: Washington road map
Licensing: Washington Freshwater Fishing License and Catch Card; Columbia River Salmon/Steelhead Endorsement

Directions: Washougal River Road follows the river and provides good access all the way up to Washougal Hatchery at about river mile 20. To get there, cross the Columbia River on I-5, then take Washington Highway 14 for 26 miles. Turn left onto Salmon Falls Road and drive 3.5 miles, bearing left, then go right onto Washougal River Road. There is bank access on the lower river at Hathaway Park. Bank access is also available at the Washougal Hatchery, located on the North Fork about a mile up from the mouth. Anglers can park there and walk or drive upstream and fish on national forest land.

THE FISHING

Bank anglers after fall chinook salmon typically fish with bait under a bobber—mainly salmon eggs or sand shrimp. A corkie and yarn setup is also a typical rig. Anglers after coho salmon use traditional gear and spinners. Washougal River summer steelheaders typically use bobbers and jigs or drift sand shrimp and eggs, while a jig floated under a bobber is a favorite rig for winter steelhead angling.

Index

About the Author

The author of, among other books, *Fishing Oregon* and *Outlaw Tales of Oregon,* Jim Yuskavitch has been a freelance writer, editor, and photographer since 1993. Prior to that he was associate editor of *Trout Magazine,* the national publication of Trout Unlimited. He lives in Sisters, Oregon.